D1637359

CHILDHOOD IS A VERB!

WHY A VIRTUAL CHILDHOOD ISN'T ENOUGH

BENTE GOLDSTEIN

To my mother and her mother,
Unni and Bente Marie, to whom I owe everything

ACKNOWLEDGMENTS

I would like to acknowledge the contributions that the following people made to my perspectives and hence this book:

My mother, Unni Bjermeland, who understood—before almost anyone did—that TV was an inferior way for kids to learn.

My grandmother, Bente Marie Bamle, who understood that "small children are happiest when they don't even know that they exist."

My stepmother, Susan Hellum, who ran horseback-riding summer camps for kids and saw how meaningful it was for kids to relate to animals.

My Waldorf class teacher, Sam Ledsaak, at Hovseter Steiner School, Oslo, Norway, because as a teacher he nourished my soul.

Our three sons, Bendik, Elias, and Hans Kristian, for allowing me to learn from parenting them.

All the friends, especially Margaret Brill and Kathy King, with whom I homeschooled several years, allowing me to ponder what kids really need to learn.

Prairie Hill Waldorf School, Pewaukee, Wisconsin, which let me be their lead teacher, graduating the kids in eighth grade that I had taught since first grade.

Dana Burns, who asked me to homeschool her daughters and with whom the program "A Week on the Farm" was started.

Anne Decker, who colored my illustrations for this book and who has been the sounding board and dialogue partner for the ideas in this book for over thirty years.

The many parents whose children attended my farm programs over the years, and understood why farm experiences were important for their kids.

My husband, Walter Goldstein, for supporting and believing that I had something worthwhile to say in this book. He helped streamline the ideas as well as edit it. Without him, this book would not exist.

CONTENTS

SECTION 3: MAKING A MORE BALANCED FUTURE

INTRODUCTION

This book is about growing balanced, healthy, happy, capable and grounded kids. It is about the indispensable ingredients that are needed for constructing childhoods that will accomplish this. These ingredients include real-life, meaningful, 'doing' experiences that build relationships with the real world in space and time. Such experiences enable kids to know who they are and to develop confidence in themselves and capacities for taking the world on. If these ingredients are not adequately considered or used by today's educators and parents, the result can be young adults that are insecure, not sure of who or what they are, and lack will for taking on the world. This book is about how to include/integrate these ingredients into today's childhoods.

I have run farm programs for kids for two decades. I constantly see the transformation in kids when they get to do things in the real world: relating to a cow or a few chickens or sawing that dead branch off the old apple tree. Children come alive when they get to do stuff in the real world that has obvious purpose. They *connect* to a place if they can be the actors *themselves*.

It is not a mistake that small children constantly and emphatically try to tell us they want to do things themselves. For them, it doesn't matter that the outcome of their deeds is imperfect; what matters is that they get into it. Kids need to get dirty and to try sawing that branch off. Kids need to try, by themselves, to make the dessert for all of us to eat. And *we* need to praise them for their efforts. Have you seen how proud they are when *they* did it, when *they* took on the world? "Look what I made!" Launching kids is about growing their capacities, which means giving them incrementally more and more responsibility.

When life was harder, it was a natural part of the order of things that kids grew into adulthood by trying things out for themselves. Back then the necessities of life itself were the demanding educator, but nowadays in our machine-rich world, there is less of a struggle for survival. Though we are glad for that, struggling had the side effect of building grit and strong will and hammering into us the reality of our physical connectedness to everything on the planet. This is mostly theory to our children now.

We have to change that.

The problem isn't just that kids do not know that carrots don't grow on trees. That could be mended by watching a film about vegetables. They would fill in the correct answer on a test after the movie was shown. The problem is that their experience of everything in old-fashioned time and space feels less comfortable to them than their lives with electronic devices. Their home, their place to be, is preferably the virtual world.

We have created an easy-street world for our youngsters to grow up in. The consequences are that it is like pulling teeth to get kids to come back to the here and now to make their beds or help with the dishes—as if parenting wasn't hard enough already!

This book is concerned with understanding children, defining what is missing for them nowadays, and pointing to a different future for education. We cannot continue with schools that *only* value head-learning. We simply have to grasp a bigger, more accurate picture of what makes balanced humans emerge from the nebula of childhood.

It was not poor Humpty's fault when he fell down and could not be repaired. It was his educators who were asleep. It is not just that Humpty did not know how to balance well on top of a wall or that he did not know how far it was to the ground. It was the fact that he had become an egghead on top of a wall and was totally unaware that he was one!

All parents have the deepest desire to help their children grow to know themselves and build capacities for living fulfilled lives. This book is about broadening our understanding of what children are like and our concept of 'schooling' for our kids. When we understand what makes kids tick, we can remedy the above scenario.

We will contemplate what is so special about kids, and how to work with them in a way that is fair to their needs. In the iPhone world of today, it is critical that we understand how electronic inputs can steal away normal childhood development. This book's ultimate objective is that we learn how to counterbalance those inputs.

Section 1

KIDS 101

1. WHAT IS THE SIGNATURE OF BEING A KID?

Kids vs. Old people

First, let's grasp the unique status of childhood by contrasting kids with older people. Children always have been busybodies who cannot sit still. They run around poking their fingers into things. Old folks sit still and their body movements become less sudden, less active. An older adult has many things to think about, many experiences that need pondering. For them, movement is happening in the hidden land of the mind. As we age we change from being outwardly awake and mobile to being inwardly awake yet hopefully still mobile. Until things fall apart at the end of life, we have progressed from living outside to living more and more inside ourselves. This is significant.

It is in the nature of things that childhood entails achieving real experiences in time and space. Being an actor on life's stage and performing in physical scenes of life is what childhood and youth are all about. In the last part of life a person's inner life is autonomously working away, mulling things over, playing through various scenarios as if seeing a film about their own life—a film that is viewable only by the inner eye. Some parts go in slow motion, over and over again. The progression is clear. As children, we are mostly busy in the concrete, material world. Later, as older people, we are busier in our minds.

WHAT WILL MY FUTURE BRING?

THERE IS PLENTY TO THINK ABOUT
FROM THE PAST.

WHAT IS INTERESTING TO A KID IS TO PREPARE FOR THEIR
FUTURE BY BUILDING CAPACITIES IN THEMSELVES.
"WHO KNOWS WHAT WILL BE USEFUL?"
OLD FOLKS LIKE TO REFLECT ON WHAT THEY DID AND
COMPARE NOTES WITH OTHERS TO INCREASE THEIR 'WISDOM'.
THAT IS UNINTERESTING TO A KID COMPARED TO DOING STUFF
THEMSELVES!

It is an old person's fate to have to look through thick glasses and listen through hearing aids. Children generally have clear and crisp hearing and excellent eyesight. It's the same for their other senses as well. We are born into this world with fabulous sense organs that allow us to check out what is going on here.

An old person has a hard time learning to speak another language, especially without an accent. Not so with children: they swim into a language without effort and come through it in short time with perfect dialect and grammar.

An old person has a hard time changing his or her habits. Not so with children: they are open to whatever is presented as the right way to do things and quickly adapt to new routines. Old dogs, on the other hand, have a hard time learning new tricks.

Children are naturally curious. They want to try things out and to see what this world has to offer them. Children, by nature, are gullible and eager to do everything. Most old people have shut doors to what they consider not worth spending time on. They have tried this or that, feel they have little time left, and cannot be exploring everything anymore. They found their topics of interest.

A grownup wanting to take an afternoon nap is incomprehensible to young children! Why would anyone want to just lie there?

The natural state of children is being sense-alert and inwardly open. Those two traits, being good at using the senses and being curious, are obvious assets to learning. The sense organs are tools for 'research,' and natural curiosity leads them on. They can touch and smell and see things first hand. Not that much knowledge transfer from us is necessary if there is an environment to learn from, as kids will learn just by the fact that they are kids.

Being Inside the World

When are kids really the happiest? They are the happiest when they are *all inside* what they are doing, fully delving in and being a purpose-filled participant inside the scene of action. Kids love feeling part of things! They want to belong and to feel they are seamlessly woven into the fabric of life itself. Kids want to find their place in this 'fabric'.

Kids don't come to join the world so they can watch it from the outside. They come here to find *their life* and *their destiny*. Watching from the outside is something old folks do; those who already have done many thing and now can sit and reflect upon it. Older people have a need to compare their own experiences with those in other people's lives. Because they also have lived their own selves 'out' in doing many deeds, they are now satisfied with the action part. They have proven themselves.

When people are older, they can live into other people and situations better than when they were young. Through all their firsthand experiences, bruises and thrills, they have gained a sense for how this or that experience would feel for a human in general. Therefore, they can bless the young better than the young can bless the young! They are now in the stage of life where they are gaining an overview. Kids are uninterested in overviews! They want to poke and squish and taste this world. They are looking for *their life* to unfold.

The general order of human development is experience first, reflect and connect the dots later. Kids are busily checking out their environments with all of their excellent senses while learning what their own limbs can do. How could they otherwise know what their own arm and leg can do?

Summary of Chapter 1:

The outer movements of a child become inner movements as an adult. Outer sensing and doing becomes inner thinking and reflecting.

Physical experiences become memories in their mental landscape. 'Experiencing' in time and space is by nature the natural (and powerful) 'topic' of childhood, but inner life will come on the heels of outer life. Life is made that way.

Inner consciousness and wisdom are the final gifts an old person can give back in exchange for an adventurous life.

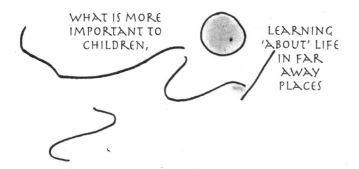

WHAT IS MORE
IMPORTANT TO
CHILDREN,

LEARNING
'ABOUT' LIFE
IN FAR
AWAY
PLACES

OR PARTICIPATING 'IN' LIFE
HERE AND NOW?

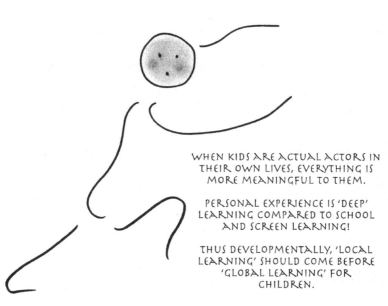

WHEN KIDS ARE ACTUAL ACTORS IN
THEIR OWN LIVES, EVERYTHING IS
MORE MEANINGFUL TO THEM.

PERSONAL EXPERIENCE IS 'DEEP'
LEARNING COMPARED TO SCHOOL
AND SCREEN LEARNING!

THUS DEVELOPMENTALLY, 'LOCAL
LEARNING' SHOULD COME BEFORE
'GLOBAL LEARNING' FOR
CHILDREN.

2. HOW DO I FIND WHO I AM?

The Will

There are elements to being human that need to be understood and fostered if we are to be savvy about how to raise kids. One of them is the human will and how it is connected with healthy individualization and development. We may not have thought about this, but children arrive here with the unarticulated question: "Who am I?"

When someone dies, that someone becomes an invisible entity. This entity is then no longer attached to a body. We say that the person 'passed on'. We see that there is no will, no movement coming from a dead corpse. In contrast, after a new child is born into the world we witness another individual unfolding in front of our eyes. The invisible entity or "I" of the child gradually reveals itself as the child crawls around poking at things. Who that child is becomes more and more apparent through its actions.

Everything we do in the world, especially with our hands, gives us feedback on who we are as individual people. Our personalities cannot but flow out through our hands and bodies. When you wrote in cursive for your teacher, you could see your own deeds flow from your hand. Your subconscious experience was: *That is from me. I am here since I can see what I have done.*

We call this elemental force that is behind every action we do our will. Our will to live. We are mostly very unaware of this will force. We take it for granted, especially when we are healthy and everything is in order. But there it is: When you press your fingers into a piece of clay, you make an indentation. You can see your fingerprint. That will-force from within you came out, and form manifested in earthly matter. What is inside you as intention got real. Your *own will* became visible in the clay. That felt affirming. You, actually, would not have known that you had it (this will) inside yourself, if you hadn't seen that mark that your fingers made in 'the world'. All of our lives we make prints outside of ourselves into hard and fast matter. All of those 'prints' are wakeup calls about how we ourselves exist!

WHICH WORLD CAN KIDS CONNECT TO?

"I MADE THAT HOLE.."

A KID DIRECTLY CONNECTS TO THE PLANET IN THE SANDBOX. OUR TABLET KIDS MISS THAT CONNECTION.

WE DO NOT GO INTO THIS WORLD BUT BACK INTO OUR MINDS.

WE NEED TO ASK OURSELVES: WHICH WORLD IS MORE REAL TO OUR KIDS, THE VIRTUAL WORLD OR THEIR OWN BACK YARD?

Think about it: if you carved your name into a tree trunk when you were a kid, what were you trying to do, really? Imagine that you just scratched "Tom + Lisa" into the public toilet door. *Why* did you do that? Were you trying to make something truer than if you didn't indent it into

7

the earth's surfaces? Did you want your love affair to be more real on earth than if it just stayed in your mind?

The prints you make in the material world are proofs that you are here as an active verb. That verb is you. Life continuously gives you opportunities to be a verb. Being a verb is being alive. Being a noun is being dead, because the happening was in the past. When things become noun-like, deeds are finished. Only the product or print is left from that activity. Seen from this point of view, life means transformation. When that verb activity stops, life itself stops.

We have to ask: what kind of sense would I have of myself if I never had printed my will on the outside world? If I had *no accomplishments* to refer to, would I have any ideas about who I am? Every time we did something in the physical world, we forged some of our own will into matter. The invisible part is the potential or *intent* to do. That forging, pressing, or expressing of our will made the invisible part of ourselves visible on the planet. It became visible for the world to see. Only when the deed was accomplished and 'pushed out into' the world could we be sure that we really *were* here. The proof of your own existence is literally in the pudding, if that is what you made.

Imagine for a moment that you are a kid cutting up carrots for lunch. You cut, cut, cut, cut, hard carrots but maybe you even cut your finger. Then, when you saw your finger bleed, you fixed it with a Band-Aid. You continued cutting carrots, cut, cut, cut. You served the carrot salad to other people. You saw them eat it and get filled and satisfied by chewing up your work. You just had an impact on yourself (cutting yourself and fixing it with a Band-Aid), on other people, and on carrots. All those experiences spoke of your own will. You experienced yourself and your environment. You experienced how and what your own body could accomplish and how you could practically make the world work. Your will was *in* the practical world, not outside it.

When a person experiences even the simplest impact of their actions on their environment, they experience themselves as being a purposeful actor within the larger context of the world. But for anyone to *do themselves right* in this world, they need to have learned and to have gained respect for the world's laws. This includes the strict laws of physics (knives can cut people), and also social laws for how we relate to each other (people are happy and grateful that you made them food).

The Experience of Ourselves

When we say "I" in reference to ourselves, we point to our invisible self. The *me*, that invisible entity that is apart from others, comes into the human form made of flesh and bones and blood and nerves. We all have a more or less conscious experience of something individual and invisible that *is* us, since we have a pronoun for it.

A child has the first experience of this invisible self around three years old when, for example, she stops calling herself Emily and replaces it with "I." This big event signifies that the child's *experience-field of themselves* has moved from her own *outside* (with you who called her Emily) to her own *inside*. Inside her own body she (for the first time) can experience her own invisible entity. She progressed from a blurry sense of self meshed into the bigger fabric, to experiencing herself a bit more individuated! Emily's invisible entity is more '*in*' when she can say "I" referring to herself than it was when she called herself Emily from the outside in. She matured a bit when that transition happened!

A CHILD FIRST EXPERIENCES BEING ONE WITH EVERYTHING

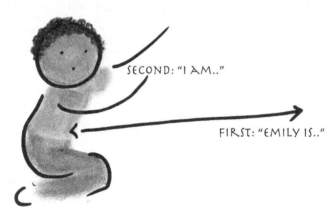

SECOND: "I AM.."

FIRST: "EMILY IS.."

EMILY EXPERIENCES HERSELF FIRST AS PART
OF THE ENTIRE ENVIRONMENT.

SLOWLY, SHE CAN SAY 'I' TO HERSELF. SHE
GRADUALLY EXPERIENCES A SEPARATION OF
HERSELF FROM THE ENVIRONMENT! HER SELF
IS MORE INSIDE HER BODY AS SHE
'INCARNATES'.

Educating the Will

Chopping wood is not just about surviving on planet earth. It is also about experiencing oneself as an alive verb of being a chopper. The wood-pile, well stacked, is proof of a person's activity, visible for all to see. "I was here, and I made a dent." Was I good or bad at it? The better my "I" was matured and grounded, the better I assessed my own abilities, the task itself, and was skillful and strong, the better the job was done.

Childhood in earlier times meant practicing making better stitches, improving hitting targets with arrows, and so forth. It was about learning earthly laws and thereby connecting and aligning with everything. Often we have no idea that we can master something until we *have to* master it. Then the surprising *hidden will* comes forth. After the fact, we are often glad for the difficulty that we had to *will our way through*! We now know ourselves much better. "We shall overcome" means willing and striving to get to new levels of stretching our will and endurance. There is no other way to find ourselves than being drawn out by something that is difficult!

Therefore, we need to provide *many different kinds* of tasks for kids to do so they can be drawn out and experience themselves as multi-capable-verbs. There is no other way to get to know oneself than doing something for real. When the real circumstance arrives, you see what can come forth from yourself. Life itself can 'draw' you out or good teaching can 'expect' it out of you.

E ducere, the Latin root of education, literally means 'out draw'. Real learning happens when something is drawn out from oneself to meet something in the 'world'. Real learning is two-fold: it is a meeting of the world and the self. The self comes forth to meet this 'world'. Therefore real life and good education can both contribute to better knowledge of oneself. The crux of real learning is that something of a person's individual flavor is invisibly 'drawn out' to make an impression in the world!

Summary of Chapter 2:

Since 'the experiencer' is of an invisible dimension, we cannot experience ourselves unless we see some proof of it on the outside of ourselves, physically.

We get confirmation that we exist (and that we are capable) when we see deed after deed making 'footprints' behind us. I made that, I helped him, and I climbed that high!

Thus kids see their will manifested when the outcome of their deed can be viewed after the fact.

They know themselves a bit better after each deed is done in the physical world. The child's invisible self comes out through a push/pull interaction with its surroundings.

CHILDHOOD 101:

I AM BECAUSE I SEE THAT I AFFECT THE WORLD.
I HAVE POWER. I NEED TO FIND THAT POWER!

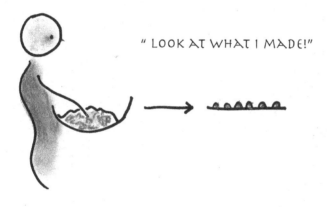

" LOOK AT WHAT I MADE!"

"I DID THAT!" WE SAY TO OURSELVES ONCE A DEED IS DONE AND WE CAN VIEW THE RESULT.

THE COOKIES MADE BY A KID ARE 'PROOF OF THE PUDDING' THAT THE CHILD AFFECTED THE WORLD. THIS GIVES AFFIRMATION.

3. WHAT IS WILL, REALLY?

Taming the Will

Because kids are generally more into doing things than reflecting upon things, it is exhausting to watch them. Anyone who has watched two-year-olds can testify to that. They are busily immersing their own actions into the bigger happenings of their environments. Watching kids can be a real challenge for grownups, because children are often fearless and don't yet know how things work. How many times do we have to tell them, "Be careful—that's dangerous"? How little effect does it seem to have with some kids? They just don't listen! They were buzzing in their own will and couldn't hear us.

Something wild and unformed comes out of the toddler. We say, "She is willful." On a daily basis we are trying to curb disasters from happening to our little one as she bumbles about. We naturally try to civilize this will by adjusting the actions of the child to fit our family's expectations and society's expectations. Teaching a kid not to spill his soup or pull down the tablecloth is just a part of what needs to be learned about what our culture allows. Such teachings are also, of course, about how to survive.

Will is this energy or force from the inside to do things, many things. The will comes from deep inside the child. Initially this will is not well adjusted. Will has to do with health and vitality. A sick kid hardly has the energy to get into trouble. As soon as health is restored, the exploring of the environment begins again, and we grownups are challenged to watch him or her. The more vitality in a kid, the more energy is demanded from us to redirect or even stop the kid's actions. It is necessary to stop their energies from flowing over reasonable boundaries to protect them.

As adults, we are happy to see small children thrive as they live and explore, but their wills can be very inconvenient at times and even embarrassing for us, too. Have you carried a screaming and kicking toddler to the car when he didn't want to leave the beach or park? At those moments, you may have wondered if there was an art to avoiding screaming fits. You were dealing with the will of the child. He is so "strong-willed," we say. It's *his* will against ours. Reasoning with a toddler usually has no effect.

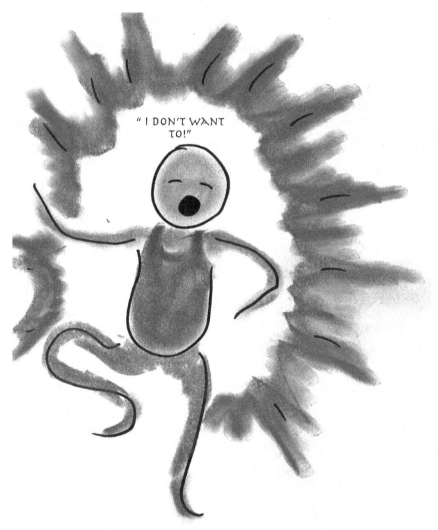

WE GET EMBARRASSED BY UNRULY, STRONG-WILLED KIDS IN PUBLIC. BUT HAVING A STRONG WILL CAN BE GREAT ONCE IT IS CHANNELED. PARENTING IS REALLY ALL ABOUT FUNNELING OUR KIDS' ENERGY INTO POSITIVE THINGS.

Our educational challenge is how to adjust this will. We have to meet the child's will with the appropriate 'forming' process to somehow make it work *within* the environment, not just for itself. Growing up means that one's own will needs to learn to tango with all the other wills out there. We grownups want a socially well-adjusted and capable boy or girl who will succeed in collaborating with others as well as the surroundings. This, as we too well know, can sometimes take a few adjustments and painful experiences.

As parents we want our child to gain abilities to do many things—sports, relationships, academics. This also takes a lot of will-training, will-adjusting, will-pruning, and will-practice.

The educational lingo for this is motor development and social maturity, but it is also, in part, about the personal will fitting into the wills of nature around him or her. It is about getting along. It is about not getting hurt by the knife's sharp edge by holding the knife right. It is about playing by the rules in a ball game and learning to master the ball. It is a difficult thing to control the ball (with its unruly round shape), but learning to control it means achieving a level of power over difficult things in the world. A good soccer player's will has adjusted itself to being a good manipulator of that disobedient ball. That ability came only by will-training and will-strengthening, by literally adjusting the player's own will to the ball's way of moving. We know it takes hours of doing it, doing it, and doing it again to be good at any sport. The will needs plenty of practice to grow sharp and good at finding and using its power.

Different Kinds of Will

Likewise, martial arts masters are very aware of how they fling their force around as they move or fight. But physical-movement-will is not the only type of will there is. A math whiz is another kind of piercing-thinking-will. This mental will also is about tenacity, strength, and mobility. Likewise, a person with patience for other people's problems has developed an emotional kind of endurance in the social, department which could be called an emotional will.

We are born with a natural knack for doing certain things and thus our will flows easily out through that knack! On the whole, our personal will manifests easily through our specific talents, but not so easily through our weaknesses. We are all made differently.

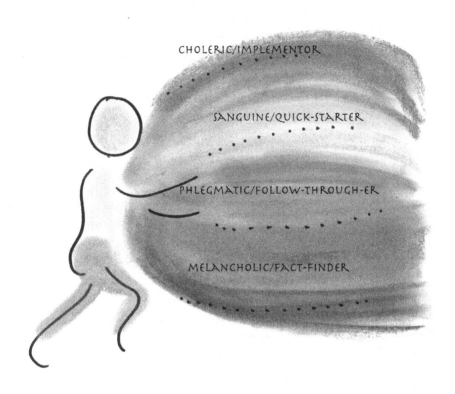

WE ALL HAVE DIFFERENT WAYS TO DO THINGS.
THAT IS OUR WILL. IT 'OOZES' OUT OF US WITH
DIFFERENT FLAVORS.
SOME FOLKS ARE SLOW, OTHERS FAST ETC.
THESE CHARACTERISTICS ARE INBORN.

WE CALL THEM OUR TEMPERAMENTS.

Some people are slow and tenacious; others are quick and lively. These tendencies or temperaments characterize how the will emerges from us. The ancient Greeks divided these latent temperaments into four groups: the melancholic (inward), sanguine (quick), phlegmatic (slow), and choleric (energetic). The modern Kolbe test (www.kolbe.com/) helps people to understand the inclinations they are born with. The same four will-tendencies that were described by the Greeks are characterized as fact-finder, quick-start, follow-through, or implementer. Kolbe asserts that the will style of each person is more or less set from the start. For example, if you are a hot tempered person, you cannot just turn that off. But all of life you can try to 'temper' your temperament.

This will, invisible and potent in nature, gets honed (or 'pruned') by interacting with the environment outside of oneself. When that has happened for a time, we get better at something. Let's characterize the capacity that was built as an 'invisible will tentacle'. Each of our invisible 'will tentacles' is the result of our will having met resistance from the environment. This resistance shaped the latent and unrealized ability that lives in the will of a child into a capacity.

For example, a soccer player's leg shoots an invisible 'will tentacle' out through a leg and a foot when the ball is kicked. After that has been done thousands of times, the leg will have a honed capacity for doing just that and will always do it right. The player develops confidence and know-how by developing the invisible 'leg-foot-will-tentacle'.

What and how much 'will' comes forth from us is very circumstantial. If something is needed, we often produce results. If a soccer player plays in a very competitive match, more effort comes forth than if the other team is a poor one. Our will and effort comes as a response to what is 'out there'.

Balancing and Growing Kids' Capacities

It's a human trait to want to balance the social milieu by playing the role that is *needed* in a situation. Teachers are often advised to seat kids of similar temperament next to each other, as they then tend to *temper* each other. Think about it: if you are a slowpoke, sitting next to another one may make you faster because you get irritated by his or her overly slow ways. This situation doesn't need another slowpoke. Because the social need is correctly perceived, another quality is drawn out of the kid to achieve social balance; in this case, to be quicker! This is the mystery of relating: As a matter of course, we naturally fill in the necessary role in the social fabric we are in. Our will adjusts to the context it was in, and often we didn't even realize that we did it!

Each role we played and each need we filled when we were children developed a capacity in us as we grew up. 'Will-pruning' or 'will adjusting' occurred for any type of job—writing, chopping wood, sewing, jumping or being polite—that we had to take on. As life progresses, we automatically grow and develop by accumulating capacities each day, building new capacities, new skills, new invisible 'will tentacles'. We are meant to grow *into* life with our participatory will. The capacities we build are *our personal answers* to the world's asking, pulling, and needing. We tango with the wills of the environments and we fit ourselves into the whole! This may occur automatically or not so automatically with a stubborn person.

'Owning' the World

When we acquire a capacity for doing something, it is as if we *take* or own a bit of the space around us. I tell the parents when kids have worked for a week on our farm that *their children own this farm now*. Our arms and hands, especially, are incredible living tools. When we use them they become *visible* tentacles, infused with the invisible will from ourselves. When kids try, probe, struggle with and acquire the skill of, let's say, cutting up carrots with a knife, their inner juju comes out through their working hands. The result is that their hands learned (literally) to *handle* things.

As our hands *handle* things, they penetrate something in the space around us. This can be accomplished by cutting carrots, stacking wood, or pushing buttons on a keyboard. All of these spheres of penetrating something in space around us are areas of skill-building for ourselves. If we got the carrot cut, the wood stacked, or the letter written, we correctly and appropriately *penetrated that piece of outside world*. We came *in*, and we came into *our own* as we did the task. We penetrated the outside world with our will and thus connected with the world. Our unpruned, invisible will tentacles were shaped by the laws of this world. This 'shaped', invisible will tentacle is another word for a capacity. A will-tentacle as well as a capacity can first be seen when the will interacts with the 'world'.

The penetration of space around us by our own will is highly significant. The more space that we learn how to 'penetrate', the more real self-confidence we will have in this world of space. It is like taking land in an invisible way. We are *taking* space by penetrating space.

A person good at a sport, will be spatially more self-confident than one who is not because they can maneuver their body perfectly within space.

We are 'space-takers', 'space-penetrators', or 'imperialists' in the context of our will life. We *have* to be.

For children it is exactly this world of concreteness and developing their own power in it, that is of interest. This is the *only* world that can affirm to the kid that he or she exists in the flesh. The physical world answers children's questions about themselves and allows them to find their place on the planet. We all have to have a place on earth to exist. When we *take* space, such as taking the court in a ball game, we show how we penetrate the space around us with our own will. This is a power experience of the self in this world. This is why people have always been interested in sports and why basketball players such as Michael Jordan or Stephen Curry are heroes! Sports heroes are masters at maneuvering their own will within the physical world of space and time.

The Inheritance of Capacities

We were all born into families with certain skill sets and into cultures with certain capacities that were already developed. I was born into a family of teachers, so I got some teacher-inheritance handed to me for free. You may have tree-cutters, doctors, or carpenters in your family, and you absorbed certain traits from them without any effort. If your family were builders you may see things more easily from a house-building point of view than others. You might handle a hammer with ease because that was what everyone did in your house. As a child arriving into such a family, you naturally absorbed a lot of those skills. Such capacities may be taken for granted. Our wills already were shaped *for* us by the common culture that we swam in. We could call it a kind of will-osmosis. Every time in history gives some 'osmosed' capacities for free. Children that have been born recently have an easy relationship with technology. It is as if they already know how to use electronic gadgets!

Different cultures naturally develop different capacities due to the outer circumstances that surround them. If we could see these 'invisible will tentacles', we would see how different an indigenous herdsman in Peru would be compared to those of us living in the iPhone world. The herder would have finely developed senses all alert to the condition of his animals. We, in contrast, would be gone into our minds, traveling far away in virtual land! Certain capacities are inadvertently built to meet the surroundings we are born into. These skills are like 'invisible clothing' given by the surrounding culture. But the invisible will-skills are invisible unless there are circumstances that allow them to come out. That capacity or lack thereof, is the proof of your level of development. If an indigenous person lands in a technological culture, there may be no use for their capacities. That person may experience a lack of purpose unless they can develop new will-tentacles, new capacities.

We are Asleep in Our Wills

Will comes out of the subconscious areas of ourselves. We are, in a way, dreamily asleep as we do things. Nevertheless, we feel strongly that *our unconscious will is us*. In a way it is almost sacred, since it has to do with our life and our destiny. It is *how* we do things. We can look at our deeds, after the fact, and be more conscious. We reflect: doing x worked but y didn't work. Though doing z was easy for me, the others didn't like it when I did y + z, etc. But conscious reflecting is very hard to do *as* we are doing things, since the *buzz of doing* overshadows reflective activity. When we are engaged in a will activity we are *inside* something. When we reflect we are more removed from it. Children live naturally more *into* the world. Therefore, we can say that children live more in their will than adults do.

Summary of Chapter 3:

Will is an invisible, inner capacity that becomes visible when we do things in the concrete, outer world.

Because a young person lives more in their senses and in their tactile experience of themselves in space, they need to have experiences of their will manifesting in the outer physical world in order to gain assurance that they themselves really exist.

Children naturally want to take hold of life physically and mentally themselves. They proudly find themselves through their actions and want us to see every accomplishment, because that is how they find out who they are.

A child needs to accomplish many kinds of deeds to grow capacities and find out about what they are and can do in the world.

Educating the will and building capacities are primary educational challenges for parents, families, and cultures.

KIDS ARE BORN AS INVESTIGATIVE 'JOURNALISTS'

TASTE, SMELL,
HEAR, SEE   TOUCH

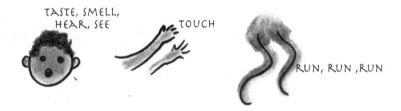

RUN, RUN ,RUN

KIDS' SMARTS ARE IN THEIR SENSES AND THEIR LEGS AND ARMS
AND FINGERS. WITH THESE 'TOOLS' THEY INVESTIGATE. THESE
BODY-PARTS ARE THEIR TALENTS!

KIDS HAVE A REASON TO BE BUSY WITH THESE PARTS, RIGHT?!

4. FIRST-HAND EXPERIENCES

Sensory Experiences

Adults must allow kids to have basic first hand experiences of this world. In fact, *sense-based learning is much richer* for children than any knowledge transfer ever could be. Knowledge transfer gives perspectives, but the senses give flavor to their lives, not just on the tongue but on their skin with every soft or rough touch. An apple in a kid's mouth is a superior experience relative to information about apples transferred via electronic devices, books, or oral descriptions. Only after the apple is fully experienced with the sense organs can other apple perspectives become valuable.

The intensive use of our senses makes all of our lives richer. But a little kid is much more of a sponge than an adult. A child absorbs everything *into* itself. It is as if it is fused with everything it senses. It has no way of shutting it out. This is why things experienced in childhood are so much stronger and have more of an impact than things that we are exposed to in old age. The surrounding materials, tastes, colors, and sounds matter much more to little kids than to older individuals because the experiences go in much deeper. We could almost call smells and tastes and all the things in the surroundings a kind of 'food' that the little absorbent sponges soak up inadvertently because they must.

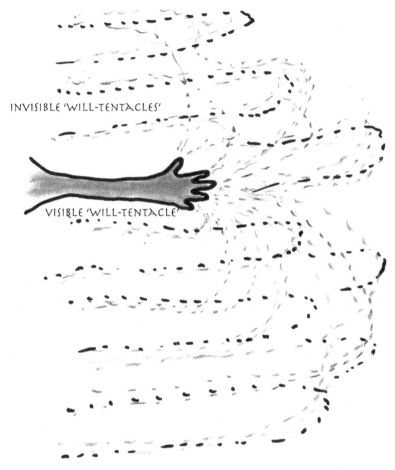

INVISIBLE 'WILL-TENTACLES'

VISIBLE 'WILL-TENTACLE'

OUR ARMS AND LEGS AND OUR SENSE ORGANS
CONNECT US TO THE WORLD AROUND US IN BOTH
VISIBLE AND INVISIBLE WAYS.
WHEN WE SENSE, WE PASS 'THROUGH' THE SENSE
ORGAN OUT TO THE OTHER SIDE! (WE DO NOT STAY
INSIDE THE ORGAN UNLESS THE ORGAN IS
MALFUNCTIONING.)
FOR EXAMPLE WHEN WE SMELL, AN INVISIBLE
'WILL-TENTACLE' GOES THROUGH OUR NOSE TO
UNITE WITH THE ODOR.

Because the child is so sense-sensitive, its universe becomes totally different depending on whether you provide its crib with a fuzzy acrylic blanket or one made from the skin of an animal that ran around in the woods of Alaska. Since every touch, smell, sound, taste, and sight goes deeply into a child without reservation and without control, *every sensed thing in childhood becomes home.* Sensations fuse the little person to its environment. That's how kids work. For kids it's all about what they *get used to.* Kids use their entire selves as they sense and absorb. They get used to things they do and experience through all their sense organs because they *used* themselves. Those exposures and interactions, by necessity, also become what they will love later in life.

As educators, we must seriously consider the sense-organ superiority that children have over us. Their talent for absorbing everything exists for a good reason. If we want children to learn to love things, we need to expose them to these things so they will acquire a taste for them. This applies to all sense experiences.

Typical first-hand experiences for children may, for example, be: learning to do a cartwheel, building a tall tower with blocks, sensing that Grandma has special feelings for them, picking flowers in the garden and checking out a caterpillar. All sensing happens *in the Now*, not later or before. Children live in the here- and-now, fully engrossed. As was mentioned above, children that are totally *in* the experience are the happiest children—to the degree that they are unaware of themselves. My grandmother who was a kindergarten teacher used to say that. Only later in my life have I realized how profound that statement was.

But if you live in your senses and forget that you exist, where are you actually living? You actually live outside yourself *inside the experience* you are having. That is a kind of paradisiacal state of being. Little children live outside of themselves in such blissful states. They are one with the world. As we mature, we gradually have to lose this bliss and union with all that is. Being allowed to be one with everything for as long as possible makes the child have invisible roots to a place that it can call home.

A BABY IS NOT 'ADJUSTED' TO THIS WORLD YET.

RUDOLF STEINER SAID THAT THE SMALL CHILD
IS AN 'ENTIRE SENSE ORGAN'. THAT MEANS
THAT A LOT OF UNDIFFERENTIATED 'WILL-
TENTACLES' OOZE OUT OF A BABY!
AS THE CHILD ACQUIRES CAPACITIES OF EVERY
KIND, THE 'WILL-TENTACLES' GET PRUNED AND
SHARPENED INTO CAPACITIES USEFUL FOR THE
TACKLING OF EARTHLY THINGS.

Since the invention of clocks, we have been cutting up the here and now into little pieces. The *'Now'* gets confined into a small mark on a clock instead of the *Being*-experience that it is! If they can choose, children prefer big, dwelling-in-it experiences.

The hectic, cut-up pieces of time that our modern rat-race offers children are not conducive to living in the *Being of Now*. Dwelling-in-it experiences give kids time to settle into themselves so they can sense all there is in their environments. Kids need a calm mood to start an intelligent nerve-sense-process of communing with their environment.

The feeling of just being able to live into things in an un-rushed way makes a kid's sensitive sense organs start to open. Through these sense organs, they live *out* in their surroundings. As soon as a kid knows that he has to leave in a few minutes, he pulls those sense-tentacles in again. Many parents have noticed that kids need warnings a while before leaving a place; otherwise, they may feel violated. Visualize their invisible 'sense-tentacles' moving in and out like an anemone!

The kid-thing is to be *in* the experience all the way, not thinking *about* it. Thinking about it means that they are not *in* it anymore; they are on the outside of it. Being and doing are both verbs where we '*live out*' our selves. When we reflect on things in our minds, we have created a *distance to the experience,* or the reflection would not be possible.

I repeat: the kid-thing is first to have no distance between itself and the environment. Children need such experiences before they can want to have distant, reflected experiences in their minds. This close contact with the world is allowed by deep sensing.

Awakening to Bodily Experience

When a kid acquires a new capacity, he has penetrated an area of life. A kid learns to climb a tree. He has done that with his own 'tool' which is his entire body. Learning about their own bodies and what they can both do and sense is a major part of children's agenda for exploring the world around themselves. There is no other way to figure out what their own bodies can do other than by plunging *in.*

We cannot instruct children about their own bodies. They have to "do the body" themselves to know what is available to them. We only provide opportunities, the backdrop, for children to find themselves as bodies with sense organs included. These are opportunities for kids to experience things *for themselves.*

Kids literally 'sift' the world *through themselves* in a personally meaningful way as they sense the world. Their own sense organs flavor the experience they end up having. That is because the sense organ belongs to *their* body. Their body likes peanut-butter-jelly sandwich or a nori roll, depending on what their taste organs got used to.

Thereby, the sensory world anchors us and grounds our invisible self into this world. Our senses are openings in ourselves by which our own invisible entity meshes with the surroundings. If we do not sense, we are not sure that we are here! The fact that children are better 'sensors' than us should be taken seriously! Sensing is their 'anchoring device' into reality!

Sanity

"He came back to his senses" was the term people used when they wanted to express that someone became sane. Becoming sane has to do with using earthly senses to verify things. Otherwise, mental states can deviate into crazy places that, literally, do not "make sense." If a kid sensed very little as he grew up, we could wonder if insanity could sneak in more easily. One thing is for sure, the senses make us sane, because the senses (despite how personal they are) tell us more about truth than our minds can by themselves.

That we 'incarnate' means, literally, that our invisible core enters the flesh in a good and grounded way. Coming *into* the 'carne' is what we see our children do as they grow up. The flesh is made of earth. Our invisible experiencer isn't. These two different paradigms, the physical and the non-physical, have to come into harmony. This *joining* or incarnating happens gradually (and mysteriously) through childhood.

An adult is supposed to be 'all here' on the planet, and in balance. Adults are supposed to understand the world they live in, know themselves and know what they are good for. Adults should be able to direct their lives with purpose under the circumstances they live in. Firsthand experiences help children to grow the basis by which they can direct their own person with better adjusted and grounded judgments, overcoming the fact that we are all knuckleheads and airheads on some levels!

Summary of Chapter 4:

Kids like to be verbs. Besides being busy as actors, they are the happiest when they live in the environment through their senses as 'absorbers' or sensing beings.

They need calm and safe surroundings to do that perceiving. Adults can help children to have these experiences.

Firsthand experiences help kids to get a first-person-relationship to their bodies and to this world. These experiences provide a firm basis for a balanced inner life as an adult.

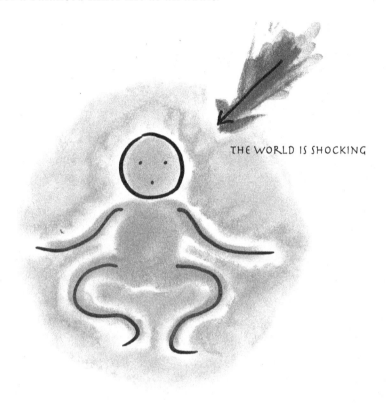

THE WORLD IS SHOCKING

NEW PEOPLE, LIKE BABIES, SHOULDN'T GET 'KNOCKED ABOUT' TOO HARD BY THE ENVIRONMENT.

ON THE OTHER HAND, IF THEY NEVER GET A CLUE ABOUT HOW IT WORKS IN THE HARD PHYSICAL WORLD, THEY CAN STAY IN BABY-LAND TOO LONG.

5. CHILDREN PLAY

Let's continue our exploration of the specialness of what children are by considering their life of play. I used to wonder if a kid could be born without knowing how to play, but I have not found one yet. Children play naturally and creatively and they love to play. Using their own imaginations, they move around and manipulate their toys, making physically visible to themselves (and to us) the mental dreaming that is happening in them.

But why, really, do kids love this activity? In part, playing means personally relating to sensory experiences that are overwhelming. In their fantasy they freely move around phenomena in their minds, instead of remaining stuck in the hard-and-fast experiences of the physical world. The physical world is ruled by the strict laws of physics. Social laws of our human culture are also strict. There are a lot of rules and laws for children to learn and absorb while growing up. To play means to move these experiences around in the world of imaginations. This is a freeing experience for children. Play is actually the only area of life where they can feel that *they are in charge*!

Play as Awake Dreaming

Kids *should* be the directors of their own play. Imagine if we grownups had someone else direct our dreams at night. Our nightly adventures could not progress according to how our own subconscious minds work. The natural play of children during the day is no different from what nighttime dreaming is for adults. In our dreams we try to sort things out!

In contrast to the free-feeling that kids have when they truly play is the bound reality of their physical setting. The branch broke when their bodies were too heavy for them to sit on it. The knife cut a finger and blood gushed out when they weren't careful. Dad got mad when they tried his razor.

Play as Therapy

Yet, in their play, they can heal the angry Daddy experience by having Dolly get the scolding for using Daddy's razor instead of themselves and by having Dolly get a Band-Aid when she cut herself. Likewise, they can comfort Dolly, in place of themselves after Dolly fell off a branch. The kids' free mental life affirms and internalizes these original experiences and puts things aright so they can be tolerated. Thus play is a freeing experience as well as an inner feeling of being alive and playful. We adults, as well as children, experience a kind of inner fount of creativity welling up inside us when we play. Play flows and streams out of us. We can wonder where it really comes from.

'Mere Play'

In the era prior to our own, children played, but they also watched grownups do meaningful and often survival-type work all day long. Acquiring food, for example, also needed the kids' participation as soon as they were able. They needed to help grow and make food, shell seeds, muck out manure, or become skilled at hunting. There wasn't that much time for just fooling around in "mere play," which was a term that people used to use for referring to kids' pastime which was thought to be useless. Helping out practically around their homes gave children basic personal experiences about life itself. Work was the heavy part of life. Play, on the other hand, lifted them above that heaviness.

As we have stated above, children naturally want to experience their *own* lives. They also want to experience the larger fabric of life and how their own little life fits into it. They are here to find out who they are in this world, here and now and what their future might be. The way they come into this world is by sensing, participating (working), and digesting their experiences as 'sensers' and doers.

Play as Digestion

Kids *digest* their experiences at night, in their play, and when they are sick. Digesting food or impressions are both ways of making something our own. We integrate a foodstuff or an experience into ourselves, and thereby affirm that we matter. Digestion is a protection 'mechanism' to integrate what we take in so that we can maintain ourselves and be whole and healthy. Not being able to digest our foods give us indigestion. Overload of impressions will do the same.

WE GET A TUMMY ACHE WHEN WE EAT TOO MUCH
OR THE WRONG FOOD!

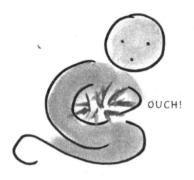

OUCH!

KIDS ALSO GET EMOTIONAL INDIGESTION WHEN THEY HAVE
TOO MANY NOT-WORKED-THROUGH IMPRESSIONS!

A LITTLE MORE UNSCHEDULED TIME USUALLY HELPS.

Play can be likened to the digestive peristaltic movements of our intestinal tracts. Where do all the digestive juices come from? They arrive just in time to deal with things! The miracle of digestion in our intestines is a natural bodily response to eating. It is no different with play and dreaming. These are life processes inside us that transform and make things healthy.

Play flows out of kids in the most natural way. All is well when kids can play!

Where is the Source of Play?

The source of play is no different from an artist's source of creativity. Because kids have so much life in them, the creative life forces are used for play. But play stops when the emotional environment becomes rushed or fearful! The fountain of play, though invisible to our outer eyes, is like a snail that can go back into its shell if touched by something threatening.

Adults have observed kids playing with their toys on the floor for millennia. They can ask, "Is play mental or physical?" In other words, when playing, are children living on the outside of themselves in space or are they inside themselves in their minds? With little children, both are one and the same thing. Little kids live both inside and outside themselves without knowing that inner and outer reality could be separated. That is why the Santa experience must be both physical and mental simultaneously!

A grownup artist, on the contrary, knows that with deep inner effort something that was inside is now being revealed on the outside. The artist has a clear distinction between inner and outer.

Play and the Subconscious

A kid's work of art signifies more about themselves than what a grownup's may do. A kid cannot separate what they are going through personally from what they depict in their drawings. The drawing is also not as interesting to them as a product as it may be for a grownup, but it is important to the child that the artwork is *seen* by the grownups. The process in the drawing was meaningful for the child *while the child was doing it*. That is because something in them informs them that "this shows what I'm going through!" The truth and state of internal affairs is thus affirmed by the drawing.

Children don't *have* a subconscious like adults do. It could be said that they *are* their subconscious-in-the-making. They are making, creating, and transforming all those traumatic causes that our imperfect

31

childhoods entail into a subconscious. Digesting experiences is a big job of the subconscious-in-the-making. And *that* is what we call 'mere' play!

Playing puts kids into a dreamlike and creative state. This state allows a mysterious flow of inner images that metamorphose like our dreams at night. It is natural for kids to play their dreamy inner mental lives out into the space around them. There usually isn't a planned outcome. This or that little item becomes something that corresponds to what is happening in the child's imagination.

Role-Play

Sometimes, children imagine that they are someone or something else. We call that role-play. Kids naturally do this role-play. "I am Mommy, and you are her fish." Kids pretend not to be a kid and try out the size of being a grownup. They try to act it out and do just what a grownup does. This living into and trying out being something that they experience outside their own person is what is natural for children. For example, the child may be a fish swimming, wiggling on the floor, feeling how it must be to have little fins for arms. This is serious business, being a fish on the floor. This is practicing empathy, being other-centered, or not self centered but rather *trying on* other people or creatures! *Children can't do enough of this activity.* By trying out these various roles, they learn to relate their own sense of self to all the possible ways to be in the world through their gifted child-intuitive state.

CLONK, CLONK..

BRUSH, BRUSH..

WATCH, WATCH..

WHEN A GIRL IS TRYING ON DADDY'S CLOTHES OR BRUSHING
MOMMY'S SHOES, SHE IS TRYING OUT THE ROLE OF BEING
DADDY OR BEING A SHOE POLISHER.
WHAT IS SHE 'PRACTICING' WHEN SHE DOES SCREEN TIME;
BEING A MOVIE CONSUMER?

Children are amused by this because they know that they are *really* neither Mommy nor a fish, and so it's humorous. "I'm not Mom, and I'm not a fish." That's why it is fun to try out these roles. When a child tries out the fit of some other being, she at the same time feels herself to be a human being relating to this or that other entity. "Mom or fish is there, and I am here. Between us we relate to each other." When a child tries out being a fish, she finds out how different she is from a fish. By doing that, she gets a clearer sense for who she is in the contextual setting in which she lives. It is a liberating experience relative to being stuck being a little kid.

Play Builds Relating

Play is very serious business. If children do not get enough of it, they don't *relate* enough. Learning to relate to other things outside of themselves gives kids that free feeling that is characteristic of play. Play is also the state of sensing their own aliveness as the creative fount flows from within. The flowing of this fount parallels the experience of their own will's streaming forth through them, whereby they are connecting with their own muses that stand behind that process.

Play is a Means of Finding Themselves

Children literally find *themselves* and what can come through themselves through play. Through the imaginations that well up inside them, they find how they relate, inwardly and outwardly, to everything around them.

Descartes proclaimed, "I think, therefore I am." Obviously, Monsieur Descartes experienced himself in his life of thinking ideas. He lived in his mind. A healthy child usually is not interested in an intellectual life, but rather living more in pictures and relationships. A child's way is more, "I dream-play, therefore I am!" A child is trying to find himself, and the only way to do that is by relating to everything around him. Kids find out how they fit into the fabric of life through relationships, where they stand in between other things, socially and physically. Fitting themselves into life dreams itself out in play.

"I RELATE,
THEREFORE I AM."

WHEN THE RAIN AND I MEET, I GET WET.

I LIKE THE SUN,
IT WARMS ME.

I AM BIGGER
THAN THAT BABY.
I DON'T WEAR
DIAPERS!

I CAN
RUN, THE
PLANT
CANNOT!

THAT PUPPY LICKS ME!
THAT IS WET AND
SMELLY FOR ME.

EVERY INTERACTION A KID HAS GIVES
FEEDBACK ON WHO HE IS IN RELATIONSHIP TO
THINGS IN THE WORLD.
A CHILD FINDS ITSELF BY PLAYING ROLES,
RELATING TO MANY THINGS AND FOLKS.
"DO THESE THINGS LIKE ME?"

"I CANNOT FIND MYSELF IF THERE IS NOTHING
TO RELATE TO!"

Play And Work

Therefore, for kids, role-play is not *mere* play. This play activity clarifies the child's inner sense of self, and that is dead serious. Role-play doesn't only happen during playtime, though. It *also* happens when the child does a chore—sweeping the floor, setting the table, feeding the cat. Real, practical roles are practiced with the child in the worker role. The difference between work and play is that in play kids decide, kids are the boss. When kids do actual necessary work, the world with its laws is the boss that decides how things are to go. You cannot sweep the floor just any willy-nilly way and get a good result!

Kids clearly need to play, but kids desperately also need to try out bits of real work. How can they otherwise gain an inkling of what is coming? Role-play and 'role-work' are both needed, the former to make things tolerable, the latter to get real. For the responsible parent or teacher it is the ratio of these activities that matters and that differs for each age group. After a child is nine years old they need chores to ground them physically in time and space. It is not about 'what I want' anymore, but rather about beginning the long road of practicing what 'the world wants from me'!

Summary of Chapter 5:

Play is necessary for kids to digest everything they experience through their senses into an integral and 'fused' part of themselves.

In play, a child experiences their own creative fount from the inside dealing with the difficult as well as easy aspects of living on earth. Play is the vehicle by which children can develop empathy and creative relationships.

Our lives are lightened by art which always has the element of play in it. The balance of play, which comes out of ourselves, and work, which is dictated by the world, is, of course, the art-form called: living.

KID-MADE 'FORT' IN THE WOODS

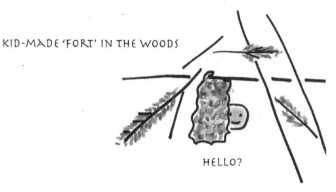

HELLO?

HAVE YOU EVER NOTICED THE
GUSTO WITH WHICH KIDS BUILD
THEIR OWN FORTS IN THE
WOODS?

THE PERFECT PLAY FORT: BUT DID YOU
NOTICE THAT NO KIDS ARE PLAYING
HERE?

WHAT IS LEFT FOR KIDS TO MAKE WHEN WE ALREADY
MADE SOMETHING PERFECT FOR THEM?

6. HOW DOES MENTAL LIFE ARISE IN CHILDREN?

We all want our kids to be mentally smart but there is a difference between smarts that arise out of ourselves and the inserted 'knowledge' acquired from a movie or a book. So how does a healthy mental life arises in a child? And how, specifically, does it arise in such a way that the children feel that they *own* their inner life?

Mental Life Emerges

Mental life rises naturally out of activities that a child performs and in which he or she is immersed. That fact is as sure as the fact that cream rises to the top of the milk, or that oil rises to the surface of water. The point is that all of us internalize our experiences and problem-solve them internally, whether we want to or not! We do this all the time because we are made that way. We are constantly connecting the dots and trying to understand what is going on in our world through our mental activity. We do this both together with others and by ourselves.

Let's say that one day a child sees a ship at sea. The child may make mental images of the ship and dream about it at night. It may reflect upon it during the day too, maybe in speaking with others. A ship was seen. Why was it there? What was in it?

Wondering is the open, natural state of children. We see and do things and then we ponder them, in that order. If the order is the other way, our inner lives become something forced from the outside in and we are not sure whether our inner life is grounded in ourselves.

Outer Life, Inner Life

We are made to have two lives—an outwardly experienced sense life and an inwardly invisible mental life. The former used to be public and the latter used to be more private. "Die Gedanken Sind Frei": my thoughts are free, is what an old German song proclaimed. That was from the time when individualistic, enlightened people knew themselves through the self-won inner content of their minds.

Truth And Fantasy

Thoughts and reality, we hope, should correspond to each other. That goes without saying. If it is not that way, we call it fantasy. Nowadays, thoughts that do not mirror the actual truth are called fake, meaning that they are lies or semi-lies. The truth has nothing to do with what we want ourselves. It is all about how the rest of the world works. From an adult perspective it is childish to be untruthful (because children slowly are learning the difference between fantasy and reality), and it is irresponsible to not think the truth. Adults feel that a catastrophe is waiting to happen the longer we wait for the truth to come out. But night, in the personally made 'movies' we make in our dreams, we are still trying to sort out the truth, albeit translated into a fantasy-rich, picture-story-version.

Children, especially before they are 6-7 years old, live deeply in their fantasy-play consciousness. It is not lying for them when they are "off" in how they render a story, like it would be for an adult. Grownups often tend to misunderstand the untruthfulness of little kids. But kids only gradually grow out of the dream-like consciousness that enabled things to transform into new things.

How 'untruthful' a kid seems to be depends on how much life force there lives in his little body. How rosy are his or her cheeks? If the child is on the paler side, they are usually more 'accurate' in their story renderings. Life force makes things grow and change. This transfers to the 'new' version of the story the child is telling.

In the midst of living in the transformation chambers called their bodies, little children love to hear the same story again and again. This gives security in the midst of all their growth.

Thinking is a Hare, Life is a Turtle

The material and social worlds have slow but very sure laws, but our thinking moves quickly. In our minds we are often surprised that the building project took so much longer to finish than we had imagined. That signifies that hardly any of us are good enough at imagining all the aspects and tasks that changing physical reality entails.

Our imagining has a wishful and willful element to it. We would like the construction project to be accomplished immediately, and take no longer. Our wishful inner nature gets irked by how tediously slow completing a job turns out to be. The physical world demands more patience and grit than the inner world of our minds.

Getting Real

Rudolf Steiner claimed that it is first at the moment of death that we become completely real about reality. But we all work and strive to 'get it' throughout our lives as we bump up against things and get corrected by the physical and social circumstances out of which things are made. Perhaps our own life force itself makes a cloudy buffer between ourselves and external reality? In any case, it takes work and experience to synchronize our lucid minds with the actual reality of concrete planet-life.

Balance

Sanity is a self-won human trait, but it is best accomplished in a community that constantly 'corrects' self-delusional concepts and ideas. We know that our minds can easily take off on pleasurable or wishful flights. It gives us reprieve from the drudgery of doing chores to survive. Our songs and music do the same. They lift the spirit so we can endure and live our lives on this harsh earth. But this blissful uplifting needs to be complemented by something that grounds us in between. Not too much of the one or the other: some fantasy or levity to uplift our inner lives, some realistic gravity to ground us in our physical environments.

Growing Children's Mental Lives

As a culture we are fond of our mental lives. We want our children to have lots of mental life. We have loaded our schools full of mental stuff for our children to get the easy way, since we have pre-sifted it for them. But for children to 'own' their inner lives, each factoid, formula and conclusion needs not to be just memorized but to have arisen out of their own activity.

Everyone wants to understand. If we present our children with *descriptions* of a problem or two, the kids will inevitably, both consciously and subconsciously, work on having their solution-thoughts arise out of the totality of the experience. Again, this is just as true and natural as the fact that cream arises from milk!

This is an ongoing process for all of us. We all wish to feel free in relationship to our own sensing and immersion in the world. The specific human thing is to rise above our circumstances and to have free thinking be the crown of our lives. Animals cannot do this. We, unlike the animals, stand up physically on two legs instead of four. This is a gesture of wanting to have an overview. In like manner our inner life wants to rise in liberating thought above its sense and will activities that fuse us to our surroundings.

CURIOSITY AND SMARTS DEVELOP IN KIDS
WHEN THERE AREN'T ANSWERS FOR
EVERYTHING!

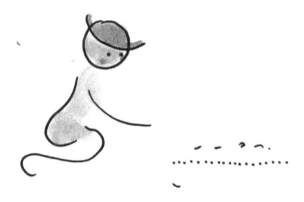

KIDS NOTICE THE INTERESTING LIVES OF SMALL CREATURES.
HOW IS IT TO BE AN ANT?

THE CAPACITY OF INTELLIGENCE OPENS UP IN KIDS WHEN THEY CAN
'WONDER'.

We 'tickle' children's natural want to understand when we let them wonder. We stop their natural state of wonder by shoving too much information their way. Thoughts that arise out of themselves are always the best, since they light them up from the inside out! We call them Eureka moments. If a childhood is full of a variety of Eureka moments rather than cramming moments, the young, emerging adult is probably going to believe in their own thinking capacity.

Educators and parents tend to fear that children will not learn to think and will not become smart, unless we stuff them full of other people's thoughts and findings. Such thoughts and textbooks may be totally irrelevant to the lives of these children there and then. But a thought that helps illuminate a person's plight there and then is much more interesting and useful to us all.

In the face of today's information age we need to understand that children need to be allowed to do a lot of self-arising thought-processes by themselves, or their inner lives will be 'owned' by the information (indoctrination) source, whatever it may be.

We used to think that thoughts should be the 'free' part of ourselves, but our thoughts are only free, when they are self-won. Mental life that is inserted into the mind, like some disk being played, is not different from an orthodox religion's doctrine!

As children advance towards puberty, more and more questions need to be put to them, not answers. We have to trust that the ability to problem-solve will come forth from the children. This mental 'muscle' or capacity is what we want to develop. In today's world, a large, 'pre-cooked' body of accumulated knowledge is available through the internet. We do not need little professors walking around carrying all these facts in their heads anymore.

I AM LEARNING SO MUCH
ABOUT THINGS FAR AWAY.

THE SCREEN SHOWS US OTHER PERSPECTIVES ON
THE WORLD.
THAT IS GREAT ONCE WE HAVE OUR OWN!

HMM..

HOW COULD WE FORGET THAT KIDS DON'T HAVE
THEIR OWN VIEWPOINT YET?

Summary of Chapter 6:

Healthy mental life arises out of experiences as surely as cream rises from milk. Truth and fantasy, to begin with, are intertwined, but separate as children age.

Mental life always has a tendency towards being too quick and superficial. Realistic thinking is the basis of sanity, and gaining it is a life-long process.

Problem solving is inherently human. Training the human mind to think can best be done by stimulating children to wonder about things <u>before</u> the answers are given to them.

Wondering, which is a natural state for children, is the beginning stage of their own self-won thinking capacity. If they get to live out their own timing in the growth of their thinking, they will gain the pleasure of aha moments.

Adults need not put all the mind content into children. In fact, giving too much information to children puts a cap on their wondering. Then the 'muscle' of their thinking doesn't get a chance to develop the way it was meant by nature.

The thoughts of children want to arise naturally out of the nebula of their unconsciousness. We are made to free ourselves from experiences and then put meaning into them through this inner distancing.

If children have plenty of rich experiences, this inner separation of thought from experience, will take place at the right time. If thinking is not self-won, but rather inserted into them, we have to call what's in their minds the content of indoctrination.

7. CHILDHOOD BEFORE
AND NOW

Nowadays we tend to think that kids didn't 'learn' anything before school was invented. That is because we think that knowledge that is self-grown and self-harvested takes too long to become much of anything! We adults have to decide for children what knowledge needs to be about and is worth practicing. Then, first, do we call it 'learning'!

When life was hard and more hand to mouth, the name of the game was surviving. We think that *surviving* is not part of 'learning' for children. We call it trauma or child abuse, and worst of all is child labor. Learning in classrooms *about* surviving, though, may be included in curricula. But immersion in things isn't as worthy of the word 'learning activity' as having the ready-made concepts served up on a platter.

All learning prior to school was 'learning by doing'. In fact it was usually 'learning by working'. It was only because our culture became aware of the fact that childhood is a sacred time, that we began to view hard labor as abusive! We started to see that we have to respect the processes that are going on in the children themselves. We finally realized that maybe it was not just all our survival needs, like feeding the calves in the morning, doing the dishes and help Dad pull out the tree stump with the oxen that mattered.

We invented schools. We started to look at childhood as the time to build children up by giving them all the knowledge they would need in order to succeed in the increasingly 'enlightened' society we were building. And sure enough, the age of working with our limbs was coming to an end through the fact that machines could do all the work for us instead of human slaves.

Let's go back and look:

Old-time Social Skills

What capacities did kids of old acquire that had *social* value? Through the millennia, most cultures had six- to twelve-year-old kids do a multitude of chores. In particular, children had to learn to watch animals. Fences were hard to make, so children became shepherds and shepherdesses. Imagine being a kid running barefoot, with knitting in hand, making a curious goat get back to the herd. Imagine the fear of having fallen asleep on a tuft of grass and waking up to no sound of animal bells. Panic! Where are they?

Every culture has songs about a shepherd boy looking desperately for a lost animal, worried that it had been eaten by an animal with sharp teeth. What would Father say when the child came back with animals missing, all because he wasn't paying attention for a moment? The child knew that the family depended on these animals to survive. What a big responsibility for a little kid to have!

Such a kid knew that he was needed. He knew that he had to be watchful and awake. He had to learn to read the animals and understand their wishes, such as that they wanted to go over to the neighbor's greener grass. The Inuit boy, similarly, had to sit for hours watching the ripples on the water for a possible catch. For grownups and children alike, it was due to 'reading' with many senses, combined, that allowed them to survive on the planet.

On the whole, the capacities that kids had to develop were paying *attention in the space* around them. They also had to extend their 'will-tentacles' around their flock or onto their prey. As a result, they developed an acute awareness for things in the 360 degrees around themselves. They developed invisible 'power-tentacles' that enveloped the entire herd of animals. They developed intense goal-oriented will-tentacles so they could hit the 'bull's eye' with accuracy.

In the case of the shepherd child, much of childhood was working on learning to control a movable *body of desires* from the outside—and managing the animals' lust for better grass. The shepherd boys, really, went to school for controlling lusts and desires. Likewise the hunter boy developed a comprehensive and deeply- felt knowledge of the animals. They knew the many ways their animals lived. Girls helped by caregiving to others as soon as they were able in most cultures.

A SHEPHERD BOY OF OLD HAD TO LEARN TO CONTROL 'DESIRES
ON LEGS' ON THE OUTSIDE OF HIMSELF. THIS, IN TURN, TAUGHT
HIM 'OTHER-CENTEREDNESS' AND PERSONAL SELF CONTROL, I.E.
DELAY OF GRATIFICATION. THIS ACTIVITY MATURED HIM!

HOW DO OUR KIDS MATURE?

When you learn to control or care for something on the outside of yourself, you transfer that to your inner self as well. These kids learned to *control themselves* by learning to control the behavior of animals. Horseback riders know this better than anyone. Being in charge of animals made children learn to be in charge of themselves. By handling the lives of a flock of animals or a single horse they were inadvertently learning to hold their 'own horses'. Learning to care for other humans in their family unit inadvertently taught girls how to care for themselves as well. Though it was unnoticed and taken for granted, life forced this 'education' on the kids. They naturally matured and 'learned' their place in amongst all the other wills and ways to be.

Kids in the past worked for their families, getting water from the well or chopping wood or gathering dry cow-pies for burning. Harvesting or planting rice or other crops was done with grownups to make sure it was done right. They did not spend large amounts of time with their peers. Having large groups of kids or teens together by themselves was an ineffective way to get work done. Everyone knew that.

Childhood was about learning *responsibility for tasks* that needed to be accomplished. Kids were expected to carry the same workload as a grownup by the time puberty hit. Their limbs were long enough and had practice enough to row the boats, ride the horses, go to war, or plow the fields. The limbs had a lot of 'schooling' by the time the full-sized human form was reached. Truly, their motor skills were fantastic compared to our modern kids! Their bodies and senses (and specially their hands) had received an incredible 'education'. In the past the skills that kids had developed in their limbs and their stick-to-itiveness and reliability were what mattered. Likewise, they had developed attentiveness, could take initiatives, and care and respect others. They knew how to appropriately use tools and accomplish all things with their hands. That had taken years of practice.

Old-time Kids vs. Modern Kids

Let's be clear: today's childhoods are extremely different from how things used to be. They are more like how royal children had it while growing up. In the past children, had to participate with and contribute to their people. Social and practical skills were mostly established by the time the children had grown beyond grade-school age. Children were part of the fabric of life and knew their place as <u>contributors</u>. Today's children practice being <u>recipients</u> to an unprecedented degree.

"HERE YOU GO.
YOU ARE ALL
PROVIDED FOR!"

OUR KIDS PRACTICE THE ROLE OF BEING A 'RECEIVER' UNTIL
THEY ARE OUT OF COLLEGE. ISN'T THAT KEEPING THEM LIKE
FLEDGLINGS IN THE NEST A BIT TOO LONG?

The old-time youth was eager to be recognized by elders. The youth did not have a different culture than the older generation. People belonging to different generations may have been irritated by having to live with each other then, too, but there was no other group to belong to than the local one. They couldn't get away from where they lived, where all ages were together almost all the time. There was no escape; you had to get along with your 'tribe'.

Summary of Chapter 7:

Today's technological children are exposed to head knowledge to an unprecedented degree. They are also not 'plugged into' the physical space around them through play or work. As a consequence, modern children lack ability to do many things on the practical and social levels.

In previous times, people grew strong in the cleverness of their limbs, in attentiveness, and in caring for others. Kids were deeply rooted in their local culture that they worked and played in. Their deficiency was that they lacked broader ideas and understanding of other cultures' ways. This is often still the case in developing countries today.

8. LET KIDS BE KIDS

Why Should Kids Even Have a Childhood?

We seem to think and often celebrate that the sooner a kid gets to be grownup, the better. The sooner he is knowledgeable, the better. We, as a culture, do not seem to cherish the specific features of children, however cute we think kids are. We do not seem to notice or have reverence for exactly those things that children naturally want to be doing. The reason for this, I guess, is that we all are pretty focused on ourselves and how it is to be a grownup! We are grownup-centered. We do not seem to ponder our own childhood experiences that deeply either. If we, as a culture, did value childhood, we would pay our childcare workers much more!

We all needed a childhood, though, and we think fondly back upon it. The reason we needed a long and full childhood was that we were on our way to find ourselves. All those experiences in our most impressionable years, made us emerge, bit by bit, out of the subconscious 'basement' that is our foundation.

Childhood should be the subconscious foundation of a healthy adult life. But, somehow, if a child was not allowed to have a proper childhood they will not be able to properly grow up either. We all know immature grownups whose childhoods were compromised. It is as if childhood needs to be childish or you'll inadvertently surface juvenile behavior as an adult.

Surely, in our psychologically-savvy culture we should be able to understand that children should be fully allowed to be children. Love-bonding, innocence, and play are the three key features of being in a little physical body. We want to be 'owned' in the safe 'pocket' of a grownup out of which we can feel secure to go out to explore the world when we are ready. If the world overwhelms us too much, we get scarred for life. If we are never let out of the pouch, that is also life-crippling. The grownup that the child is bonded to should expose the child to reality gradually and gently, but surely. A little person's confidence in themselves is gradually built as this 'letting loose' from the apron strings happens in a sensitive way.

'All I needed to know I learned in Kindergarten'. We may have all heard that saying, but that is exactly it. At the appropriate time, Kindergarten activities and explorations are things that children should be allowed to focus on. The lessons for life taught in Kindergarten are profound and children need to be given time to learn them. They shouldn't have to focus on too much else. Being a kid should be about learning to live harmoniously on Earth with each other. It is that simple. The hardest thing we can do here is to learn to get along. The image of a place where kinder (children) are playing in the garden reveals a deep understanding of children! And there is a lot to learn in that 'garden'.

Speaking of gardens, growing plants is not unlike raising kids. We cannot force many things to happen too quickly. We have to let the growth tell us what it needs. Too strong a wind breaks the stalk. Too little light makes it weak. Too little nourishment makes the plant small. If we over-fertilize a plant, it will not make a strong plant either. Our job as caregivers is to tend to the growing process in a calm but awake way. Is there a more important job than this?

Summary of Chapter 8:

Though our culture does not yet fully realize it, a healthy childhood is critical for society's health because it provides the foundation for a healthy adult.

The ingredients of a healthy childhood are in harmony with what children like and most desire.

Children like to:

1) Safely grow and develop in calm places as they bond with others and are being loved.
2) Get to play out their own fantasy and imagination.
3) Be allowed to not be so self-conscious, but to live outside themselves in their environment soaking it up.
4) See themselves as 'helpers' as they participate in real tasks.

5) Get to be exposed to many things and 'flavors' through people that they can learn to love.

6) Be encouraged to wonder about things in both school and home which enkindles their smarts more than information.

7) Practice purpose and service and kindness every day.

Section 2

NEW PROBLEMS

The good side of our technology is that it is making information available on a mass scale never before experienced by humanity. But our gadgets also create obstacles for children to have a healthy childhood. These obstacles have never existed before.

In this section we will explore more specifically how technologies create these obstacles for our children. These obstacles arise mostly in the form of deficiencies of the kinds of basic human activities that are necessary for children to do in order to develop in a healthy way. These are deficiencies in the activities of movement, speaking together, growing social skills, sensing, doing chores, caring for others, creative mental activity, parental attention, development of stamina, realness, and not least in the children's existential need to find who and what they are, themselves.

As we read the below deficiencies that tablet-kids now may acquire, we should keep in mind that this is the first time in human history that this experiment of absence from physical space and time has been possible to execute. Only time will tell which aspects will show themselves to be of bigger significance as we get more and more enmeshed with our technologies, it looks like.

9. LESS PHYSICAL MOVEMENT

Movement

Our children used to play in the dirt with sticks and stones. They made themselves busy by poking fingers and hands into things. Kids dealt with the ground right under their feet and explored what they found there. It made their limbs the busiest part of their little bodies. Their limbs moved as their fingers got into things and their whole bodies followed. In a way you could say that kids' wakeful, little fingers led them in their pursuits. Their physical body moved and crawled into and onto everything. Their bodies related to everything in a prepositional way: over, under, inside etc. That took movement. In the same go their bodies got agile and developed motor skills. With all this activity they were making a life for themselves with themselves in the center of it. Children grew into life one deed at a time.

We grownups find it a lot of work to watch kids so they will not get into things that may harm them. Therefore, it is easier for us to have kids sitting still! Electronic media on screens takes care of this for us. It is the cheapest and most effective babysitter invented.

We all know that now much of this (for us) troublesome child activity has changed for our children. They do not need toys for their arms to move around like before because they are dealing with virtual things in their minds or heads instead (now portrayed on their screens). This takes hardly any bodily movement at all. This has, obviously, made our children's limbs much less active. Also their eyes move less. For example, when we watch a screen we blink only half the amount of times compared to when we look at our surroundings. Our children's limbs and bodies and eyes have become still while our clever device do more of the movement for them instead.

When kids rarely use their body as a 'tool' to explore their surroundings, they will as a consequence, naturally, know their body less.

The predominance of screen time over physical exploration time has caused many more kids' bodies to be *less* skilled than before. Kids have less motor skills not just because of too much screen-time but also car-time. Since that car moves, we do not have to move ourselves. Our machines enable our stillness. In fact, our machines have made our limbs more or less obsolete, unless we use them for exercise or sports.

From this point of view, children today are doing what old folks used to do. They sit still and are busy in their minds. There is a difference, though. Old folks have mind activities that were based on their own sense experiences from earlier in life. Our technological children have other people's sense experiences, not their own, giving them mental transfer through the screen.

THIS KID 'LIVES' IN
THE SPACE AROUND
HIM

THESE BOTH 'LIVE' IN
THEIR MINDS

=

KIDS NATURALLY 'LIVE' OUTSIDE THEIR LITTLE
BODIES IN THE SPACE AROUND THEM.

WHEN KIDS 'LIVE' ON THE SCREEN, THEY 'LIVE' IN
THEIR MINDS. THAT IS THE SAME 'PLACE' WHERE
OLD FOLKS LIKE TO BE.

THE DIFFERENCE BETWEEN A KID AND AN OLD
MAN IS THAT THE LATTER'S MIND IS FILLED WITH
HIS OWN REFLECTIONS. SCREEN-KIDS MINDS GET
FILLED WITH OTHER FOLKS' REFLECTED
EXPERIENCES.

Not moving around, not playing and fooling around, is by nature not how children behave. When kids sit still, they are physically more passive. They are inadvertently *practicing passivity.*

As a consequence of this lack of normal child behavior, geek and noodle bodies have appeared. There hardly ever used to be such bodies. This is, of course, the effect of too much sitting while doing screen time.

Sitting still for long periods of time is a totally new phenomenon. Because of lack of movement, kids are more pale than in previous eras. Because of too much watching of screens, their eyes also need glasses earlier.

Sports

The place where kids get to move around is mainly in sports or martial arts. Sports help kids to have the body movements they need to counteract our sitting culture. Furthermore, in organized sports some grownup cares about the kids, too. However, sports can sometimes get too competitive and too serious for little kids. Little kids before puberty mostly just want to explore what they can do on their own terms, not compare themselves with someone else. Competition, when grownups get to be very involved, can easily tend to get too competitive for the little ones.

Sports now are all steered by grownups and there are organized teams and events. But let's not forget that sports have replaced the time that was used for free play. We created the sports world with good intentions: to get the kids' still-sitting bodies moving. But we ended up taking away the necessity for kids to 'figure it out for themselves'. That doesn't mean that sports aren't good and fun. My point here is to make us aware that grownups are deciding what and how kids are playing and moving. Kids used to determine their bodily movements more themselves, especially in their play time.

Kid-regulated Games

When kids entertain themselves, especially the years before puberty, it is not so much about winning as just doing it. Girls and boys through the ages have played red rover, tag, and hopscotch with plenty of arguing about the rules that they all worked out together. This working the rules out, according to fairness, was good exercise for what is to come for their adult life. Most kids miss out on much of any kid-made game nowadays, both the movement-part as well as the figuring-it-out-part.

When a kid never problem solves social issues regarding fair play in games, they therefore never practice sticking their nose into communal problems. The 'muscle' of feeling responsible for social outcomes is not exercised. When kids try to work it out, they are practicing the taking hold of what feels right or wrong. That is leadership practicing.

Having A Real, Significant, And Memorable Childhood

We have removed ourselves from the natural way of life and this removal affects our children the most. We can ask whether Mark Twain could have written *Tom Sawyer* if he had watched videos most of his childhood? Could his descriptions have been that vivid if he hadn't been running around in the woods and sensed with all of his body the kinds of childhood experiences that Tom Sawyer had?

When our iPad-children grow up, will they tell of exciting things that they saw on the screen from their childhood? Most of us agree that it will not have made *that* big of an impression. And why is that?

Remembering Our Childhood

Most of what modern children will have watched on their screens will be forgotten. It did not make that much of a print *into* them. That is because it was someone else's eyes that saw what their camera recorded. What is on a screen is predigested by the film or game makers and thus does not require much neither from our children nor ourselves.

WE HAVE ALREADY
FIGURED OUT
EVERYTHING THAT YOU
NEED TO KNOW.

BUT I WANT TO
FIGURE
SOMETHING
OUT!

WE THINK THAT TEACHING MEANS THAT
WE HAVE TO REGURGITATE EVERYTHING
GROWNUPS HAVE FIGURED OUT UNTIL NOW
TO OUR KIDS.

DON'T WE SEE THAT THE KIDS GET MORE
PLEASURE BY FIGURING OUT A FEW THINGS
FOR THEMSELVES?

Furthermore, our consciousness on the tablet is half dreamy; involved in dreaming other folks' content. Outer physical experiences with the body's entirety of sense organs will have a stronger, wakening impact on us than a film ever could have.

That which doesn't require much *from* any of us will not make much of an imprint *on* us either. We remember always better what we ourselves did, compared to what is given to us for free. Whatever we struggle with, will stick. Because we have to struggle, we experience the world in a stronger way. We also experience ourselves more. We get to know our own will and deeper layer because something was difficult. This is a law.

Watching a video or fooling around with it is 'easy street'. In contrast, having our own experiences, creating our own inner mental pictures, and doing things ourselves actually has more significance *to ourselves* compared to a mind-inserted movie. There is a proverb that goes, "I will forget what I heard, I will remember what I saw, but I will *know* what I did."

Summary of Chapter 9:

Little children's bodily movements are the outer 'show and tell' of children wanting to do things in the world themselves. Movement itself, both self-directed and learned, is a fundamental and groundbreaking effort for children to conquer everything here in life. Virtual childhoods result in less movement and less skillful bodies.

Sports can help children to move. Physical games regulated by children themselves often end up being more age appropriate than grownup-led sports.

Being in charge of their own play time also calls on kids to develop their sense of fair-play and creativity.

If we want to live our own memorable life, we need to do things that make us move our bodies and express our will through it.

Our kids are more passive and have less memorable childhoods because they move less. Movement and life itself are connected.

10. LESS SPEAKING TOGETHER

Speech vs. Pictures

It goes without saying that speaking becomes unimportant when a picture can convey a thousand words. And do we have pictures to show! We show each other our photos and things that we find online and laugh and have fun. Seldom do we bother do all the explaining that it would take to convey whatever it was we saw on the screen.

Little children used to 'hang on every word' that came out of a storyteller's mouth. No longer is that the case. In fact some children cannot even get much to happen in their minds when words are all they have.

We can wonder if the great classics will be read by the masses in the future. We live in a culture of quick fixes, and many of the greatest literary works are tediously long. It is surely much more tempting to go to the ready-made image than do the detour via the words, since mental images is what we are after anyhow. Because of this, we have a new hurdle to overcome for reading teachers. Watching the movie compared to reading the original book is like eating candy and sugar compared to eating a wholesome meal from a dinner plate. All in all, the screen-activity takes away a refined mental imagining-activity in ourselves that we may hardly have been aware of before.

Speech Wakes Us Up

Speech pathologists will be in high demand to serve the abundance of overly screen-addicted kids that result from our technological advances. Research on kids, adults, and electronic media show that if grownups are involved in watching media together with kids, kids get more real and serious about it. If parents watch with their kids and especially talk about what was seen afterwards, the content is naturally incorporated into real life for the children. Children need this help. It helps their world to get whole and helps their language develop. Words from the grownup are bridging the mental with the physical world for them.

Because adults contribute words to the screen-experiences that only an experienced speaker and 'word acrobat' can muster, the benefit for the inexperienced speaker is invaluable. For two reasons this is very helpful for kids' learning: their own *language develops* and it helps them to become *more awake* to what the content of the media or what the real event was about. When we are more awake, we are freer in ourselves. If this word-setting doesn't happen, what was seen remains more of a dream to children and grownups alike. Words, simply, wake us up more than pictures do.

Dreaming, from this point of view is an 'immature' state of consciousness. The picture came before the abstract word. We see this principle manifested in the history of writing itself: picture writing came before symbol writing.

But just as our childhood is (and should be) spent more in a dreamy, blurry state of consciousness, screen experiences are also dreamy. But what happens in childhood and also through pictorial media activities are formative to a high degree. The screen inserts its dream into us and works into our life from the subconscious and up into our actions. Because this is slipping into our minds so easily, it works more strongly than consciously articulated words and stories. When we make our own mental images from words, we are, after all, using our own life experiences as 'paint' for our pictures. This is absent when we watch the moving pictures on the screen, and thus it is more like an indoctrination than words ever could be.

THROUGH MEDIA, IDOL AND KID MERGE TOGETHER.

THE IDOLS MATTER FOR WHO THE KID WILL BECOME LATER.

WHAT KIND OF HEROES DO YOUR KIDS HAVE?

ONES THAT DO SOMETHING GREAT OR ONES THAT 'LOOK' GREAT?

Advertising

The advertisement industry understands the power of pictures better than anyone. As soon as we talk with our students about how that dandruff shampoo advertisement tries to make them all feel that they have to buy it in order to be a confident person, it loses its power over the kids and ourselves alike. When grownups claim that they turn the music off and don't pay attention to the ad when it comes on, they show that even they do not understand how that ad works! It is exactly when you do not give the ad any analyzing attention with your word center, that it has power over you! When you think of other things than the ad when it is in front of you, it actually goes right into your subconscious. Most likely you'll buy that brand next time and you will not know why you just got that one. You just *felt* like it.

That is exactly why speaking with kids is so very important. Bullying in school loses much of its power once it is talked about on a daily basis. When we stop talking about difficulties, these social problems can become much bigger than are necessary. The fact is: the less we speak about things the less free we feel.

Speech Resolves our Problems

This is one of the great things about our times; we can speak about many taboos that were impossible to bring up before. Words are helpmates that give us distance from our problems and place all experiences into relationship and perspectives. This is exactly what humans have going for them! Putting words on things was what Adam was supposed to do. The first man on earth, according to our human origin-stories, named things. The animals did not have that job, but we did. We were supposed to get an inner overview that only naming things can give us. The *consciousness* that arose from that naming was our human contribution to the creation-processes on earth.

Speech Makes Us Free

We could say that it was a gift to the verbalizing center's development before there were no pictures available anywhere. The stone-age man made some simple pictures in the sand or on a stone wall. The only way to convey an experience was by describing it. The teller re-experiences in a slower way the entire sense experience he had and 'works it through' as he re-lives it mentally. The story that everyone hears is imbued with the personality of that person. The teller literally got to ex-press, press out in word-codes, his inner life. After we have 'unloaded' a story or an experience, we feel lighter and freer, right? When no pictures of our vacation were available on any phones, we had to re-live in our own words and cathartically 'digest' our experiences. This was healing as well as personally validating.

Summary of Chapter 10:

When we speak, we bring a higher and more awake consciousness about in ourselves than if we just show each other pictures or movies. Words make a more awake consciousness than pictures ever can.

Since it is more laborious to put all those words on the event we experience, we are greatly tempted to show our phones instead of speaking all those sentences.

We develop our children's speaking less each time we show a picture instead of using words. Verbalizing events and feelings alike help us not only with our communicating, but also problem-solving.

We are also gaining an inner sense of freedom as we have 'unloaded'.

11. LESS SOCIAL SKILLS

Together Alone

'Together-Alone' is the blurred state of neither being fully together nor totally alone. We sit together but we are on our phones doing something else. This common, socially accepted mind-body disconnect is now the new norm. In daily living at work and at home we often have to sit in our own worlds, each on our own devices, because that is how the world works. Out of necessity, parents' attention is often on their phones, not with their kids. Children sit next to their parents, and they are also pacified with their device. Everyone is somewhere else than with those who are around them physically.

Technology brings us closer in one way, but at the same time it makes more distance between us. It has become acceptable that bodies sit together but that minds are elsewhere texting or talking to others. People start texting someone else, even, while you are talking to them sometimes. We are all being drawn out of the here and now continuously. We all experience how it is very hard to resist.

The Impact Of Together-Alone On Children

When kids are physically alone in their rooms, they are together with their friends on the phone. When they are physically together with their friends, they can feel very alone not knowing the latest message popping up somewhere behind someone's back. This could be the case before, too, of course. This painful part of social life has now gotten to be amplified by telecommunication devices.

In fact, the danger is that our electronic communication-devices make barriers and new types of misunderstandings for healthy relationships between our children and their real peers. There is an enormous pressure for kids to be 'on' as they constantly are checking their cell phones to know what is going on in their virtual social scene.

The truth is that most grownups would not want to know what is going on in an 8ᵗʰ grader's life, actually. Youth used to keep many of their thoughts in their diaries that were for themselves only. It is hard to keep secrets now. Since phones became life lines for preteens and teens, the slander, bullying and horrible talk that can be found amongst that age group has mushroomed. For kids it is often painful to be on the inside of the 'news' and also painful to be on the outside of the 'news'.

It is harder to hide and feel safe. Kids are channeled to become very self-aware and overly conscious of each other's daily outfits and boyfriends or girlfriends. For teenagers, this phenomenon was always hard. Now the anxiety is going through the roof.

TO BE OR NOT TO BE..

A CHILD SHOULD BE THE CENTER OF ITS OWN LIFE.
ONLY THEN CAN A CHILD BE EMPOWERED TO GET GOING
WITH ITS OWN LIFE.

"AM I THE SELFIE?"

OUR DEVICES ARE MIRRORED REALITIES

WHEN WE ARE ON DEVICES, WE DO NOT EXPERIENCE OUR CENTRAL BEING AS MUCH AS WE EXPERIENCE BEING 'OUT THERE' SOMEWHERE.

Kids Are Forgetting Themselves Less

This overly self-aware state of consciousness is also affecting the lives of smaller children whose natural state is to prefer to 'not know that they exist'. Kids are happiest when they can forget that they themselves are present, because they are so engrossed in their experiences connecting them to their surroundings. Being overly self-aware makes kids less aware of the world around them because their consciousness can only be one place at a time. We have only one field of attention. If it is focused on ourselves, we tend to freeze and stop experiencing everything else.

Forget Yourself To Find Yourself

"It is by forgetting myself that I find myself." People in all cultures had wise people who understood the profound truth of how we find ourselves: by being so engrossed in someone or something else that we forget ourselves as we totally immerse ourselves into a situation.

Self aware children are in pain, whether they are overly shy or very precocious or even acting cool. They have a sense that they need to be something that they are not, thus they freeze in their shell or act out or literally, cool down their own feelings. How does that help them in their (unspoken) quest for self knowledge?

This unnatural state of self awareness is natural to go through in puberty, but in today's world it happens much earlier. Being cool is definitely not being engulfed, engrossed or hotly interested in something. Being a child is about forgetting oneself as one is wondering and curiously investigating this world. That giving oneself over to the experience, whatever it may be, is a necessary ingredient as a child finds out about themselves as an individual. If a child has to play cool all the time, he will not get to 'play himself' but rather the cool dude who may have cooler feelings than he himself actually has!

It is for real, that when we apply ourselves all the way, we find both what the world is about and also what we are good for. Self-aware states of puberty surely are needle eyes that need to be experienced, no doubt, but let us not make that painful state longer than necessary!

Learning Good Social Skills

When kids are more 'together' in the virtual than the physical level of existing, they are living in the virtual 'landscape'. Their life energy is in the mind's inner world. While living in our minds alone or 'together' as it may be, we are inadvertently practicing *__Not Having a Place__* in a physical-social fabric. Whatever we do, we are practicing being in that setting, physical or virtual accordingly. If we are often on our devices, it is necessarily lost time outwardly in time and space, getting corrected by grownups about how people like to be treated.

Learning good social skills in physical surroundings when we are young means developing the capacity to make a place for ourselves and others in the physical-social fabric. We learn, often the hard way, manners and gestures so *others* will feel well around us. As a result, we also end up feeling much better ourselves (in general) when we make another feel pleased with us. Good social skills therefore make the world go around better because we all have learned to think of each other rather than just ourselves.

Any time spent away from the real and physical social settings can create the 'nerd' or 'geek' that just isn't adjusted well to how others work. These thin-skinned humans did not have to rub up against others to get the pointers about how people as a whole entity work. They are used to the part that can transfer through the devices, only. This is not their fault. It is the surroundings that let it happen. Most of us got plenty of corrections of our manners or lack thereof as we bumped into other folk's feelings and territories as we grew up. We adjusted and grew some 'social skin' as a result.

Practicing 'Other-Centeredness'

In earlier times, children had to be seamlessly incorporated into the life of hunting or agrarian activities as soon as there was any possibility of being useful. They were 'fused' into the 'body of community needs' and life itself. They learned to tend animals, stalk animals, kill animals, sow seeds, pull weeds, harvest plants, carry water, make clothes and tools, and prepare food that everyone shared. In such a way kids were *immediately* plugged into life itself.

We know that these tasks are now absent. Our time is spent learning new computer programs and looking at screens, and in between these activities, we are popping ready-made sustenance into the microwave. This means that our children aren't practicing being seamlessly incorporated into the physical scene where they live. There is no need for that. Instead they may learn obeying the rules of activities on-line. This may require some screen-manners, or 'nettiquette' as someone coined it, but they are often quite different from the physical manners that may be needed at a work place, for example. We live in each our own worlds and can wonder if we are all verging on the self-determined world of the autistic individual with ears and eyes all plugged into what we prefer (or can tolerate)!

TECHNOLOGICAL KIDS ARE 'SOMEWHERE ELSE'. IF WE
DO NOT MAKE SOME RULES ABOUT GADGET-USE, WE'LL
NEVER BE TOGETHER WITH OUR KIDS!

WHO, THEN, IS BRINGING THEM UP?

Children seldom practice really being there for others, though, since most of what people do on the tablet is on their own time. The screen as a place to be is allowing a much more self determined world than the physical world ever could. You can wait to answer someone on Instagram. In the real world you have to respond when asked there and then. You are 'on call' in the physical time and space. Online activities 'prod' and 'prick' you less demandingly and thus give you a 'buffer' between those demands and yourself. Though this is true on one level, the on-line social life can also do the opposite: make people feel that they are always on, that they always need to answer to things. This can make people feel that they hardly 'breathe' as they are bombarded with a message in the middle of the night as they sleep with their phones.

These days most children do not practice providing food or serving of each other. The important habit of 'other-centeredness' *isn't being practiced.* Put crassly, we are inadvertently teaching our kids that they do not matter to the other as much as before in practical and concrete life. This can lead to kids wondering why they exist at all in the physical since mental life is where it is happening. Modern kids may end up having an unspoken existential crisis. This is because they never experienced themselves as seriously needed for anything hardly ever. All they experienced was silly stuff online!

Summary of Chapter 11:

The roles we play when we are children end up developing our social habits and informing us about the kind of person we see ourselves becoming later.

If we as adults value mature 'other-centeredness' in our fellow humans, we need to arrange childhood so these qualities are cultivated.

'Screen-kids' practice being disconnected from the physical world and each other. The time spent on tablets replaces real relationships with people and nature. Electronic versions of connections are flimsier and less hard and fast and give children a more unsure social foundation to stand on in this world.

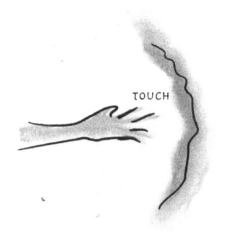

JUST AS WE HAVE SMALL LEVELS OF ELECTRICITY IN OUR OWN
NERVES, SO CAN WE SAY THAT WE, TOO, NEED TO 'GROUND'
OURSELVES ELECTRICALLY TO THE PLANET.

HOW ELSE ARE OUR 'LIGHTBULBS' GOING TO LIGHT UP!?

12. LESS USE OF THE SENSES

Screened-in Childhood

The screen brings about a kind of 'screened-in' childhood for kids. It makes a barrier between themselves and the physical/social world that exists in the room they are sitting in here and now. We are 'there and now' when on devices.

The main way the twenty-first century differs from the past is that we have a lot more technology. The clever machines we made are doing the work for us. Technology, literally, brings the world to us. We do not have to go to the outer world other than for pushing buttons. It is certainly more work going into the world compared to having the world go into us!

We have transferred both work and play into functions of our devices. Our own activity in the physical world has been minimized. Because children are so into touching things all around them, they will end up doing less touching and feeling and tasting of their surroundings. They will be having less exploration time into time and space than ever before. This exploration time involved much trouble for adult care takers, of course, and that makes our devices understandably a great temptation for young parents. How much easier to instead plop an iPad in the kids lap than to run after them…

Technology: Second-Hand Sensing

What's wrong with educational games on the tablet?

Everything kids get on screens and in schools is *predigested* material. What is different now for kids is that grownups have pre-experienced and pre-digested everything for them. Kids get very little learning happen from the original 'source' being it nature or a real human being. We have created filters (screens) through which they may re-experience *our* actual experiences. We give our children plenty of stories already pictured perfectly for them on a flat screen. They do not need to make their own mental images since the screen provides ready-made ones.

Likewise with our schools, we hope that kids will be excited about *our* experiences, and do well on *our* tests, where we check how clever *we* were in constructing curricula. Our school and media culture plainly proclaims that kids do not need to have their *own* experiences. Our technological culture is into giving children secondhand experiences—lots of them.

Learn First-Hand!

But that is not good enough for kids. Children need to have their own actual physical experiences in time and space. They have been equipped with the best senses to investigate a few things for themselves. If we ask children what is more interesting: doing something or just hearing about/ seeing it on a screen—— are you in doubt what a kid will answer? Unless a child has 'learned' that the world is a dangerous place, any healthy kid will want to do it themselves!

Truly, children today have less opportunity to learn-by-doing. Where can they get into it, really? Instead, children get our grownup non-sensing-version presented to them through the media of our choice. The end result of such a knowledge-inundated childhood is that our kids don't practice using their good senses or being curious observers. Quite the opposite, they practice only being recipients of previously acquired mental content, now regurgitated on smart boards in front of the classroom; later regurgitated in tests. Everything is based on second- or third- or fourth-hand experiences.

Overly Sanitized And Protected Childhoods

Poking and prodding and getting into trouble by doing risky things had dangerous effects in the past. Some children died in previous eras when they did reckless things like jumping on ice flows in the spring. We, quite the opposite, will not have any risk-taking for our children; instead we tend to 'bubble-wrap' them.

Kids are not getting dirty, nor scraping themselves up, never having a bee sting. They have clean, detergent-smelling clothes every day! The children themselves smell like their deodorants. In all ways we are trying to remove them from both the real world and the natural clean (odorless) smell of their own bodies by tweaking a number of natural smells.

In myriad ways we shield our children from reality's truths and inconveniences. Why?

Life in the twenty-first century does not allow children to use their sense organs as it did under more primitive living conditions. Our kids live in a poorer sense-scape than kids in the third world. A fire to cook food was replaced by "unfeelable" microwaves. A powerful and strong-smelling horse was replaced by a not-much-to-sense car. The socks made from synthetic fibers that warm our feet do not give us the same sense experience as did the fibers of the plant or animal that was used to make socks.

Since the plastic diaper is so comfortable to wear, the modern tot has no need to stop using it. The old-fashioned kid on the dirt floor or in a papoose in a skin wrapping with a not-so-even moss diaper was used to a lot more discomfort and sensing in general. All the harshness has been removed from our lives, causing us to have thinner skin towards outer, physical environments. This thinner skin causes kids to be anxious, as a natural result.

Even though we can eat all types of ethnic foods in restaurants, we have less life stuff going on in our homes—less cooking, harvesting and tending to animals and nature. How could we possibly supply kids with such experiences when we live in apartments in the city? We may have cleaner places to live, but these sterile places have less content and are less nuanced.

We have removed ourselves from the immediacy of the planet's reality. Food, for one, usually turns out to be a little different each time when it is prepared from scratch. The terroir of a food determines its taste; that is, the taste depends on which piece of land it was grown on, what time of year it is, and so on. That variation isn't allowed in commercial food production since companies have to guarantee the same taste every time.

Why are first-hand experiences important for kids?

Let's be clear: our technology is fantastic, especially for grownups. Not only does it make our lives easier, it also gives us more perspective by allowing us to compare our own lives with the lives of others. But children do not have any life basis to get perspective on as of yet. Children take the screen as their first experience at face value. If you'd never seen a real horse, but you saw one on the screen, that screen horse would be all you know. We grownups fill in a lot of sensory memories based on our smell and feel experiences when we see a horse on a screen. People with experiences with horses get more out of seeing horses on a screen than do people with no experience.

What's wrong with devices for kids?

Our sensing has been replaced by sensors in our devices. Our iPhones are doing the job that an overall alert *bodily sense system* used to do. Our own sense-based judgments aren't necessary anymore since we have these devices. Such devices are useful for old people whose senses have deteriorated. But they are atrophying our children's natural talents.

In this context, these new contraptions are an insult to kids. Think about it—do you go outside to feel the temperature or do you look at the weather app on your iPhone? You may know what cold feels like, but have modern kids been "bitten" by it yet? Do we start to run from every unpleasant experience?

Even though our own sense organs' probings into the environment may not be as sophisticated as the gadget, it is nevertheless *we* who are involved in sensing. The gadget reads the temperature, which is anyway an abstract concept for the kid who has hardly ever felt uneven temperatures in his thermostat-equipped house. The point is that we have made ourselves and our developing sense talented kids obsolete in amongst the myriad of machines. All our contraptions and devices 'do' life for us.

HAVE YOU TRIED SKYPING WITH YOUR DOG?
THE FRUSTRATION OOZING FROM YOUR DOG SHOWS
YOU THAT THE DOG DOESN'T LIVE IN HIS MIND.

DOG
SITTER

THROUGH SKYPING
THE OWNER SAYS:
"I LOVE YOU,
BUSTER!"

BUT A SMALL KID DOESN'T LIVE IN
HER MIND, EITHER!

IT IS NOT HELPFUL OR FUNNY TO A
ONE-YEAR OLD TO SAY HELLO TO
MOMMY ON THE PHONE!

Viva Sensing!

We call sensing experiences first-hand experiences. That is because our hands are the first we have 'at hand' to poke and prod at the outside world. Thus it is the most obvious and visible tentacle or 'sensor' that we have. But, in addition to the concrete arm with a hand at the end, we also have invisible 'tentacles' going out though all our sense organs. We are unaware of this and take it for granted that we smell the smoke from the far away camp fire. But out through our nose arose an invisible smell-feeler (tentacle, as I call it) that brought the information back to us. Each of us have more or less developed invisible tentacles coming out of us. We all sense away with these 'invisibilities' all over the place subconsciously all the time.

As adults we know the value of quality sensory experiences for enhancing the quality of our lives. For example, tasting good wines is a heavenly experience for adults. We don't want to lose such experiences. But sensory experiences of many kinds, both pleasant and unpleasant, have been removed from the lives of our children. It behooves us to let children develop their own sensing 'tools'. It is, after all, what we all were born with as our natural capacity to 'read' the world! Unless we give children a certain amount of sensing activity, they are bound to feel (unconsciously) that their acute sensorial 'talents' are obsolete. Kids will 'lose' these experiencing-organs unless they are used intensely all through childhood.

"GRANDPA WOULD HAVE DRUNK THAT BUG!"

WHO NOTICED THE BUG IN THE LEMONADE, JOEY OR GRANDPA?

SO WHO IS 'SMARTER' IN THEIR SENSES?

Summary of Chapter 12:

Though technology makes our lives more convenient, its application to the lives of kids prevents them from having first-hand experiences. When we remove basic earth experiences away from our kids' sensing-history, however, we also take a bit of their lives away from them.

If we allow electronic screens to tell them what kind of life they are having, we will stultify their capacities to have these first-hand experiences.

Sensing as a way to gather information is sifting it through our own bodies. That activity makes the senses sharper and sharper the more we do it.

When we sense, we enmesh ourselves <u>with</u> the world and do not feel apart from it.

SOMEBODY IS ALREADY SINGING FOR ME THROUGH MY EARBUDS

THE WHEELS GET US THERE

"WHAT IS LEFT FOR ME TO DO?"

FUN COMES TO ME THROUGH A DEVICE

GROWNUPS DO EVERYTHING FOR ME

THE MICROWAVE COOKS FOR US

WHAT ARE OUR KIDS FOR WHEN NOTHING IS LEFT UNDONE? ARE THEY THERE JUST TO CONSUME WHAT GROWNUPS MADE?

13. LESS CHORES AND CARING FOR OTHERS

Helping Out

Kids who learn to help out get 'helping out skills' built into them as habits. Practice makes masters here, too. But kids are helping out less these days, and that is often because there simply aren't things to help out with! But there are parents who do not believe in 'forcing' their kids to do stuff either. When children do not have any chances in helping out and being useful, they are neither getting certain skill sets nor any good habits. We are, inadvertently, setting them up for a hard time towards their future. How will their spouse like it when they never pick their dirty socks up from the floor or leave the dishes undone?

I tell parents that they do their kids a favor by teaching them how to do chores and to do them well, because their kids will be popular with their future in-laws. I remind parents: The kids are working on their future 'popularity' in real life.

Getting in the habit of picking up the dirty socks and putting them in the hamper when you are 32 is about hundred times harder to learn than when you were 10. The fact is that many grownups will never learn it at that later age. They will, plainly, stay in the habit of not picking up that sock. They practiced being a 'royal' that some servant (mom) should do the dirty work for. He actually practiced the opposite of being helpful, namely 'not picking up the sock'.

If we let our children not get habits of good manners, we have a similar thing happen: The kids are actually _practicing_ being brats. That is a habit of how to be! Doing chores, which is serving everyone in the family unit, is a form of learning to respect things and others. Doing chores _well_, is therefore shaping attitudes on a deep level. The child is learning to submit under the task needing to be done. The task is the 'boss' and the child is becoming more beautiful by serving this 'boss'.

Necessity Is A Good Thing!

Kids complain away that other kids don't have to do this or that. This sassy recipient-attitude was never accepted in prior times. Life was just too hard. It is true. Parenting was pre-scripted by 'Necessity' itself. Those parents weren't wiser than today's parents. They just didn't have the time to haul water and cook at the same time. They didn't have time to run to a sick grandmother with food and watch the little one at the same time. Kids that were in the grade school age-group would do the easier tasks, run the errands, and bring in water.

Responding to necessity made kids good at doing all sorts of things and it truly prepared them for what was coming. They were part of life and the social fabric in the most natural way. We may ask, why aren't we valuing our kids' getting to practice being useful? Do we really think that becoming responsible for a kid will grow all on its own?

Building Habits

When a kid does something or does nothing, they are still practicing that something or nothing. Kids are building habits by every deed they do or don't do. They are 'using' themselves, thus they are getting used to helping or not helping. In today's world kids practice being onlookers, recipients and by-standers more than participants, givers and concerned helpers. This is because *we* set it up for them this way. We adults have not understood that ***all roles of being a human being need rehearsal***.

Since our clever machines and devices are busy doing jobs for us, the work-habit-building opportunities evaporated. That was the whole point of the machine in the first place: to do work *instead* of us. The 'pulling' out of a will 'tentacle' in a human is now not needed. The many tasks of cooking food are not needed now that the pre-made food can quickly be warmed up in the microwave. In concrete terms for children, that means that the practice of cooking was taken away from them!

The washing machine washes our clothes. This took the skill away from us how to wash clothes. Because we send our little ones to day-care, older siblings have fewer chances to practice care-giving at home. Instead, the older sibling practices getting good grades and is cramming for tests for herself only. She instead practices staying afloat in the 'cool-game' at school so she will not be picked on. This is the reality of 'practicing' which we have created for our kids and we do not know how to not do school and home life any other way.

We have the idea that if the older girl or boy stayed home to practice caregiving, it would be called child labor, which is taboo. Instead, our kids practice gathering knowledge for themselves and having fun with their peers. We think that kids have *the right* to not have to contribute or 'care-give'. The understanding that kids helping, contributing and giving builds habits that will cause exactly those traits to come forth in adults, is absent in today's consumer culture.

Technology Stole Our Movements

The moving of our bodies has been taken away by the car. Think of how many leg movements all children made in prior times when they never sat in a car. Every machine has taken away a movement that our bodies otherwise would have to perform. We transferred the 'doing' to the machine. It is in the nature of our machine and technology culture to make ourselves obsolete.

Living is responding to real things in real time and space. That involves *movements* from our own bodies. What happens when kids live life, is that they move in a myriad of ways. All this movement, including appropriate responses to 'necessities' build 'motor skills' in our children's limbs. These motor skills are what we call capacities that can then give possibilities to our children's future. The better limb control a kid has, the better chances of survival and a good life they have.

We Need To Practice Caring

When a kid sweeps a floor, he learns to care about every crumb that was on that floor. He was looking at the floor, sending his own will towards the floor. Afterwards he was proud of that crumb-free floor. A task, such as sweeping crumbs away from the floor, demanded an element of *invisible care* being induced and grown in a kid however little he or she may have liked it at the moment! We made kids care about crumb-free floors by having them sweep the floor many times. The repetition of a caring deed will make also the habit of caring grow in the child. Modern kids end up caring less about their physical surroundings, simply because they do not do deeds 'into' it.

Caring about the needs of others is a similar thing. Babysitting means practicing caring for a little sibling. Practicing watching that an animal always has water and food is likewise an invaluable 'skill'. Practicing that plants get the right amount of water is also learning to care and understand the needs of plants. We should all feel the 'pain' for our potted plant when it looks limp because we forgot to water it. We develop that sensing for other living things by being 'plugged' or 'pinned' to serving that other creature.

Consumer vs. Giver Culture

We have a powerful consumer culture, but can you imagine for a moment if we had a giver-culture, instead? Being a consumer points to consuming. That activity is necessary when we are little babies. All the arrows of both attention and food go towards baby. Gradually as baby matures the arrow has to turn to be pointing towards others. A consumer-culture is therefore a juvenile culture. A giver-culture is a more grownup culture.

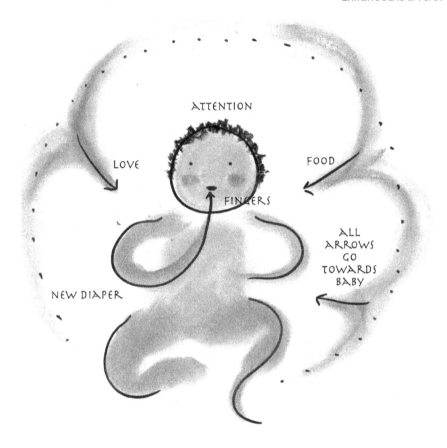

ATTENTION

LOVE

FOOD

FINGERS

ALL
ARROWS
GO
TOWARDS
BABY

NEW DIAPER

OF COURSE, A BABY IS CLUELESS ABOUT THE DANGERS OF THIS
WORLD. AS BABIES WE SOAK UP EVERYTHING AROUND US: FOOD
AND IMPRESSIONS ALIKE. BEING A BABY PRIMARILY INVOLVES
BUILDING ONESELF UP FROM EVERYTHING COMING TOWARDS
ONESELF. THUS THE ARROW IS POINTED TOWARDS THE BABY BY
NECESSITY!

ALL OF CHILDHOOD WE ARE ACTUALLY TEACHING THE KIDS TO
TURN THE ARROW THE OTHER DIRECTION, SO THAT "IT ISN'T ALL
ABOUT YOU!"

Childhood is the time when we should gradually practice growing into the grownup way of doing things. That means caring about others, not just ourselves. Otherwise we call ourselves 'selfish'. To see that our grown kid is selfish is a painful sight. Practice is what practice does. If a child practiced a self-centered childhood it will be difficult for them to evolve out of that place!

Summary of Chapter 13:

Our gadgets and machines make our kids incapable and weak compared to prior generations since they do so many jobs for them.

Because of our machines and reactivity to child-labor, kids aren't given opportunities to practice much work of any kind. They simply do not get chances to practice 'other-centeredness', neither for things in their environment nor other living creatures.

Kids are concretely practicing being in another world than the one we are all in together physically when on gadgets.

Kids are being left in whichever left-lane that they find in the virtual landscape because we are often too busy ourselves. Inadvertently, kids are practicing not to play any roles to things around them in space. That is 'autistic' in nature.

WHERE ARE YOU AS AN EXPERIENCER WHEN YOU GO
INTO SCREEN ACTIVITIES?

THE LAND OF THE MIND IS A MIRRORED LANDSCAPE
IN CONTRAST TO THE CONCRETE WORLD OF THE
SENSES.

14. LESS SELF-CREATED MENTAL ACTIVITY

Mental Visualizing

In past eras, children would be told stories by their elders. The little words were codes that stimulated the creation of mental images in each mind, thereby leading to individualized 'mind-movies' in children and grownups alike.

This kind of inner activity is hardly noticed even though it is an activity! We took it for granted. But this invisible activity actually develops a capacity: mental visualizing. If we hardly ever translate words into mental images, that capacity will be weaker. On normal tests, it would be called 'comprehension'.

(Mental images are also made from actual sense experiences, of course. We can see inwardly the landscape that we were just in, for example.)

Dominant Mind-Pictures

When most of our information comes ready-made in the form of a movie, we do not exercise the inner 'muscle' for transforming the sound of words into pictures. It is much more demanding for a person to make their own mind-movie than to receive it from a screen. The pictures from a screen movie are more dominant in their nature. If we read a book before we saw the corresponding movie, we often find that we cannot conjure up our own 'book-version' that we imagined after the movie was watched. Before we watched the (real) movie, it lived in our minds vividly, now afterwards it was out-competed, more often than not.

Regarding Fixed Or Movable Inner Pictures

The clear test on this is to try to remember what your own mom looks like. Isn't it easier to remember a photo of her compared to just her from all of life, itself? We know who she is on her inside so well that the outer version of our mom is hard to 'see' with our inner mental eye. When the photo of her comes to mind, it is fixed from one situation. That is easier to hold on to. This may show us how both photos and screen-movies have a dominant superficiality about them compared to our own mobile and nuanced comprehension of what we experience. A photo, per se, is after all only the outside surface of something taken at a fixed moment.

There are two issues to consider: 1) How dominant, fixed, or mobile a mental image is. 2) The origin of images: did they come from a camera or from ourselves?

Second-Hand Experiences

We have to ask: If all we experience is ready-made movies from screens and we hardly make our own inner self-made mental images, will our inner mental life be our own? With other words, did Hollywood sign its name on most of my 'inner life'?

Telecommunications are about communicating about something else, someone else, somewhere else, far away. So how can a tablet or phone tell a kid who they are and where they have landed since its purpose was to tell about something else far away?

In fact, the pictures on the screen of our electrical devices represent the attempts of other people to express their minds. When we see a movie or play a game, we are absorbing some other mind's version of life. It is most all from the past, because it was made in the past.

When we see a video or movie a dominant screen picture is plopped into our minds with hardly any effort on our part. This is why we feel rather un-alive after hours of watching. We were very passive ourselves as we were literally led by our eyes. Obviously, we feel more alive, the more active we are. To check the difference, look at people's eyes when they go into a movie theatre and compare that with how different their eyes look when they come out of it.

Effects Of Second-Hand Experiences On Kids vs. Adults

There are three detrimental impacts of electronic media on kids. It weakens their capacity to comprehend, it makes them passive, and it steals away their time for having first-hand impressions.

Surely, we adults can learn a lot more about the world by seeing all these images from wherever. YouTube videos, for example, are creations from other places and other people that can give us interesting perspectives that are new and fascinating for us. We think that's a good thing. But if it is too much we, too, can lose our own footing amidst a barrage of information.

But, when we are a very new child here, we do not have any first-hand experiences. The need for gaining perspectives isn't present. We, in truth, have nothing to get perspectives on yet! The younger we are, the less fruitful a flood of information is.

Training Kids To Be Led-Along

The reality of screen-watching is that we then haven't made our mind-content ourselves through word-to-mental-image activities. We also have concretely practiced being led-along.

Being led is something that most children are being in any case, but traditionally it has been by grownups, other children, or their own senses and desires. In the past there was an activity where children practiced leading themselves. That was called playing. To get to that, let's consider for a moment how childhood and that play-activity used to be.

The Activity Where Kids Lead Themselves

Kids used to entertain themselves and one another, not be entertained by grownups most of the time. But often, children had little time to play as life demanded that they help out by running errands and doing chores that they could do almost as well as grownups. When children helped the grownups, they had first-hand experiences. Kids much preferred to play, of course! When they played, they practiced allowing their inner fount of creativity to be flowing, often in collaboration with others.

In contrast, the work they had to do grounded kids. The play they got to engage in had a signature of lightness about it. It had levity. It balanced the heavy feeling of all the necessities' sense of serious gravity. In their free play they actually were supposed to practice leading themselves and determining their mental content, since their creativity was in charge.

When a child practices being the leader of their own activity by taking initiatives in their own play time, they are practicing something very valuable for their grownup state. A grownup is supposed to be the leader of themselves, right? In their fantasy-life a child can take initiatives. It is, in fact, the appropriate place to practice initiative-taking when you are a child.

This initiative-taking can gradually grow more and more into the practical leadership roles, too, as the child gets to know the world and acquires some personal know-how.

The Modern Predicament

Now let's look at what modern kids experience:

Doing art work is supposed to be 'creative self-expression'. But if art work is pre-determined by coloring books or programs on the screens, the kid is less able to express their own creativity.

Ready-made toy 'contraptions' from the world require less inner effort from kids. It is a totally different activity for a kid who pretends that a stick is a tractor and moves it around than for that kid to play with a perfect little John Deere little tractor.

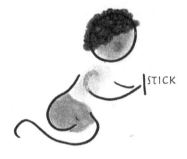

STICK

WE FORGOT. PLAY SHOULD
BE A 'FREE' THING THAT A
KID GETS TO DO.

WHY, THEN, DO WE LET THE
TOY INDUSTRY DECIDE WHAT
PLAY SHOULD BE?

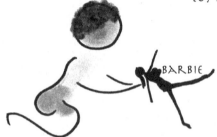

BARBIE

IF WE GIVE KIDS ACTION FIGURES
FROM MOVIES THEY WATCHED, IT IS
HARD FOR THEM TO PLAY ANYTHING
BUT RE-RUNS OF THE MOVIES!

WHEN DO KIDS GET TO INVENT THEIR
OWN STORY?

Playing is a kind of self-directed fantasy, like dreaming. Dreaming at night in bed is like a self-made movie. In our dreams we try to digest our impressions and make them 'our own'. But watching a movie is like having other people's play or dreams inserted into us.

When toys tell kids what to play, we stole their free inner imagining from them! We stole their chance to see their own 'dream' in front of themselves as they played it out.

Overloaded Kids

Much of what today's folks, both young and old, dream at night is about other peoples' movie-dreams! When we dream, we have to try to make what we saw and experienced into something that can be useful for ourselves. We are made that way: what goes into us as impressions must be made into transformed things in ourselves. We have to 'digest' it if we aren't to have sensory overload. If it is too much, we feel disjointed, fractured and not whole.

We make ourselves whole by having some of ourselves come forth and meet the overwhelming 'intruder' or 'information'. With actual food we produce intestinal juices to break it down. If we get too much or the wrong food, we get indigestion.

With a situation of sensory overload, too many impressions, we need 'down-time' where we are allowed to be more dreamy and 'spacey'. We create inner images and reflections to rise above these impressions all in our own chosen tempo. If we aren't allowed to give these responses to food or impressions alike, we will get sick. Our bodies kindly take care of our whole-making for us!

Summarizing What Children Are Losing

Three capacities have been undermined for our tablet-children due to lack of healthy activities:

1. Losses in the capacity to form one's own mental images from 'thin air' based on hearing words. This is because we are inundated with pictures to an unprecedented degree. A picture is a thousand words, of course.

2. Losses in the capacity for creative, self-made, mental play welling naturally up from the inside. The well has been turned off by floods of domineering screen images or by too 'perfect' toys and coloring books. Too hectic lives, of course, contribute to this, too.

3. Losses in the capacity to take initiative and lead, because the flowing of the inner creative fount is hardly experienced. Children today who hardly ever invent their own play end up not even knowing that they *can* invent anything!

Thus, the most detrimental effect of technological life in the twenty-first century may be caused by *what children don't do* while they are living 'inside' their electronic gadgets!

The Consequences

Few parents properly value hours of self-made play by kids. Instead, they often schedule the kids to go to some grownup-led activity. Thereby, kids in our society practice being recipients, onlookers and receivers as well as 'entertainees' their whole life, often.

This puts them into the passive position of being led, rather than leading. But if everything a person ends up doing through childhood are things that are steered by the outside world, either by physical events or by steered mental events from a screen, we have to wonder if a person isn't just becoming a steered robot, all programmed! In contrast to this, a healthy society and democracy depends on educating free-thinking, creative people.

Summary of Chapter 14:

Children have the tasks to develop their own lives. For that to occur, they need time so they can have their own firsthand experiences and their own self-created play time.

Our devices take that time away allowing less of these inner self-steered activities to occur in our children. The creative fount from within may never be experienced by kids that are hooked on tablets and other electronic devices.

LEARNING FROM A TABLET IS A SENSORY-POOR WAY TO LEARN.

ESPECIALLY WHEN THERE ARE NO FIRSTHAND EXPERIENCES TO REFER BACK TO.

KIDS TAKE EVERYTHING AT ITS FACE VALUE. IF THE SCREEN IS ALL A KID KNOWS, HOW COULD IT KNOW THERE WAS MORE TO THINGS?

ANY KID INTERACTING WITH A SCREEN COULD JUST AS WELL HAVE BEEN ANOTHER KID OR A ROBOT. CHILDREN NEED SPECIFIC FEEDBACK ON THEMSELVES TO LEARN TO KNOW THEMSELVES.

15. LESS BEING SEEN BY PARENTS

Helicopter Parents?

Kids are being *seen less* by parents because their parents are on their iPhones instead of watching their kids. Moms on phones, babies on phones, too. Despite the fact that many parents could be named a helicopter parent, it is increasingly difficult to attentively hear and see our kids.

Being seen for who they are and what they now can accomplish is what children desperately need. They don't need to be controlled where they do not need to be controlled (which is the result of parents *not really* seeing them, of course)!

Babies Need Absolute Attention

Imagine the amount of attention from grownups that kids got when their parents potty trained them before they were a year old (or 6-7 months old by the Eskimos). The constant observation of their tot, so they didn't have to change one more diaper (which meant moss picking-drying-storing) was worth it! Now that pampers are relatively comfortable for babies, we do not have an incentive to be that observant for when our kid 'needs to go'. But it was a gift to little people that they were seen almost every minute of the day!

Nowadays we have monitors in baby's bedroom to 'worry' and 'think of them' for us. So we can fully concentrate on other things until we are really needed. But little children want and need as much of their caregivers attention as possible. From a small kid's perspective, the caregiver should worry about them all the time.

Being carried, like all babies used to be in the past, aided in the feeling of 'someone is there for me' at all times. Babies and toddlers are hopelessly incapable and they naturally need us to support them all the time: physically and psychologically. They were made that helpless *so that* they would receive all our attention and care. They were made to be incredibly cute so they would naturally get that attention from us with joy.

Learning (subconsciously) as a baby that you are so very important to everyone around you, gives you the important message: I'm valuable! I 'bathe' in all this attention and interest. I feel they really want me here! Babies thrive especially well if their parents manifest acute interest in them, since this baby came 'out of' them.

Gradually, as children grow up they will learn to not need absolute attention all the time. They are satisfied and they can start looking all around at everybody and everything else. From this place they now can start maturing into that fact that life is not all about them. But that cannot happen if it wasn't all about them in the very beginning.

Kids Need to be Recognized and Affirmed

When I learned to walk, the best and most thrilling part was that I was the one doing it. When I learn to climb a tree, I called out for Mommy or Daddy to see me sitting on that branch. "Look at what I can do!" When I conquered a new skill, I needed to be seen, received, applauded, and encouraged by the significant other people who were nurturing me. Then, when I was lovingly received and seen, I was glad and felt empowered to take on my part for my own life and for things around me.

It is a nightmare for a kid to be left alone in this world! But often our technological kids feel pretty alone and disconnected. They want desperately to be noticed by some caring grownup. The typical scenario of unseen kids is this: Boys cause trouble (see me, see me)! Girls want to please or vanish (piercing and cutting themselves or worse).

The Art of Parenting

Good parents go to ball games to see their children play. If a child scores a goal, we know how disappointed they will be if no one saw them as they came into their own. For a child, this being seen is so important that they almost would have wished they didn't score, but waited until Dad could have seen them.

The fact is that when we see our children, we help them in their search to find themselves. And they need to be continuously seen as they change. A kid is always in the stage of becoming something new and that has to be taken into account all the time. A kid doesn't *equal* that bad deed they just did! A kid is on the way to learn from that deed, both about the world and themselves. If we over-define who our children are, and put them into fixed conceptual boxes, we are making a mistake. Thus we need to have an intuitive perception for the emerging person, not for just what's concretely in front of us.

Whether we like it or not, we end up giving children their self-image or lack thereof. That is exactly the difference between a grown person and a kid. We grownups should know who we are. We already have a self-image. Kids are self-images in the making. Our responses or lack thereof, affirms or does not affirm the mental image of themselves that they end up carrying around.

Thus every deed a kid does, teaches them about what they can do as their own person and what that own person is. Every deed makes them experience their own self emerging from the unconscious place they came from as a baby. When we see our kids, as they do deeds of all kinds, we can meet them as we correct and affirm them. Affirmation feels good for a kid and corrections are painful. We need to help kids correct for too grandiose of a self-image or too minuscule of a self-image. Giving kids correct assessments and balanced perspectives is part of the art of educating kids. It is a lot of work to launch a kid well.

Consciousness for all of us is a painful thing. When our inflated image of ourselves pops, we are devastated. Practicing taking a few blows and still feeling loved by our parents, is what childhood always entailed.

That is because our parents love us unconditionally and therefore some scolding can be tolerated by us. That is the gift that a good parent gives their child: the feeling of being loved and corrected at the same time while the parent's intuitive sense sees the 'who' that is emerging through what sometimes seems to be a chaotic behavior.

Grownups, in general, do a better job of seeing who a kid is than other kids can do. That is because other kids are first and foremost interested in finding *themselves*. All kids use each other to find themselves and their own power. Grownups should be done finding themselves if they are mature. Hopefully they are freed up so they can see the kid objectively.

Kids Imprisoned in Images

When kids look at themselves in the mirror it doesn't help them to see who that invisible emerging person is. Teenagers become aware of their zits. Bad hair days are invoked. Their images cause fear and frozenness, the opposite of ease and spontaneity.

That mirror image is a surface image of a person, not the potential of the person inside themselves. Clearly it is more painful to be a youth than before because kids see themselves from the outside all the time in mirrors. They constantly see fixed images of themselves in photos of all kinds.

Because they are not seen for who they are inwardly as much as before, kids can get extra hung up on cell phone photos of themselves. They can actually feel a certain death by losing that phone or if some 'wrong' picture was sent to the wrong person.

They have a legitimate fear. That is because every photo fixes a person a bit in other people's minds. Being fixed in people's minds makes it harder for all people to be ourselves here on the planet. We need other people to lure us out of ourselves, not fix us in mental boxes.

As children participate more and more in electronic-media-life, and less and less in life itself, their self-image changes. If there are thousands of pictures of themselves on the net it is very hard for them to not identify themselves with those images! That means that the children identify themselves with a noun, a photo, more than being a doer, a verb. They can feel that the 'world' owns them, just like any celebrity does.

Kids are Verbs Not Nouns

In the past, time was always filled with activities in the practical realm that supported the maintenance of human life on earth. People in the olden times were doers, and they hardly knew what they looked like. There were no mirrors or totally quiet lakes to admire themselves in.

But today's kids see themselves more as a 'thing' from the outside in and less as a multi-faceted and capable verb potential from the inside out. There simply haven't been enough situations for them to see themselves as living doers because our society hasn't prioritized giving children these real-life opportunities.

Being a verb means being the various capacities and activities that came, come, or can come out of children's bodies. But that is why what a kid can do or has done is important for strengthening a truer and surer self-image. Everything that a child accomplished in their life, namely, became an invisible 'badge' that whispers to the child: that was me.

"LOOK WHAT I MADE!"

FOR A 2-3 YEAR OLD, IT IS A MONUMENTAL EVENT
WHEN THEY DRAW A CLOSED-UP CIRCLE!

WE NEED TO NOTICE WHAT KIDS EXPRESS OUT FROM
THEMSELVES.

COLORING BOOKS TELL KIDS THAT GROWNUPS
ALREADY KNOW HOW TO DRAW.

DOES THAT ENCOURAGE KIDS?

Kid Celebrities

Many social media platforms tend to make kids, especially girls, present or sell themselves like mini-celebrities. The urge to learn to put oneself 'out there' in the virtual landscape is very intense. But if it always is about projecting an image that titillates others, our own actual person can find itself not to be seen. Young girls can want to evaporate, if this is the case!

The real self can find itself 'drowned' and unnecessary here if some other image of oneself is dominating out there. The celebrities of the world are 'eaten-up' by the millions that feel they 'own' them. A kid, on the other hand, actually should be 'owned' by just a few people, not millions.

In fact, being a child celebrity is not what you should wish for your child. A child celebrity is not allowed to develop out of themselves, like a child should, because the crowds just want the persona they know. Celebrities generally feel an enormous pressure to produce the persona the crowds wants, not necessarily the one they feel they are now. A child develops so fast that they should not be fixed in a box! Our job as educators of children is to draw out new possibilities, not fix them so that they can become something sellable for audiences.

Summary of Chapter 15:

Being seen by adults is life or death for children. Babies and toddlers need constant attention while kids all through childhood need recognition and affirmation.

We are in charge of helping kids develop their self-image. We do this by seeing them for who they are as the verb potential. We help to adjust and correct the deeds they perform to align with the 'good' kid we know. As their guardians and educators, we are asked to stand next to them and believe, and coax what we intuit they are able to develop into.

Grownups, being more objective than kids' peers, need to know their responsibility of seeing kids for who they truly are and can become.

'101 LIVING ON EARTH'

I ACT..

THE 'WORLD' REACTS..

LITTLE ME
REACTS..

THE 'WORLD' ACTS..

WHEN A CHILD INTERACTS WITH THEIR PHYSICAL
SURROUNDINGS, IT IS PART OF EVERYTHING, PART OF
THE LANDSCAPE. THE REACTIONS OF THE CHILD MATTER
AND REAL FEEDBACK HAPPENS. THE KID FINDS ITS REAL
SELF BECAUSE THE REAL SELF MATTERED!

16. LESS GRIT

Old-Time Grit

Grit is will to the extreme. A person with grit will endure and stick to the task whatever comes. If you look at the old photos of immigrants coming to the United States, you'll see this trait. These people had endurance and overcame a lot. It wasn't as if they had a choice, either. Life hadn't given anything to them on silver platters. They had to work hard for everything that they possessed, materially as well as psychologically. Will or grit is a trait that is developed by meeting difficulties and pushing through anyway. Imagine the men that built the railroads and all the times those guys lifted shovels or picks! With new machines, that work became unnecessary and it stopped. A lot of human grit-building also stopped with it when such manual work was eliminated.

Socially, people also developed more grit than we do now. Those immigrants couldn't go to their rooms to take a break from a social setting. No one had their own room and people lived in crowded settings. Private lives were not something that anyone expected to have much of. You endured what was hard and kept things inside. You had a smile on your face or a stiff upper lip, at least, most of the time.

Resistance Develops Grit

Rudolf Steiner talks about what develops will in kids. It is by giving resistance. For will to develop strongly, we have the physical metaphor of the muscle. If the world outside of ourselves resists our efforts, we often succeed only if we push even harder. It is like bicycling up a hill. You may get to the top only by exerting yourself to the max.

A good thigh muscle will evolve if you do a fair bit of that motion again and again. The bigger the muscle, the more grit you end up with in that area where the muscle announces itself. Grit can be measured physically in muscle-bulge, but most grit or will isn't to read so obviously on the outside of a person at first glance. We rather see it come out when the hard spots in life arrive.

The cars that we sit in as we drive ourselves from here to there, therefore, have stolen that grit-development away from kids. How little effort it is to push a pedal compared to walking 100 miles? We have legs that look like pencils! Folks in the olden days had bulging muscles in their legs as a matter of course.

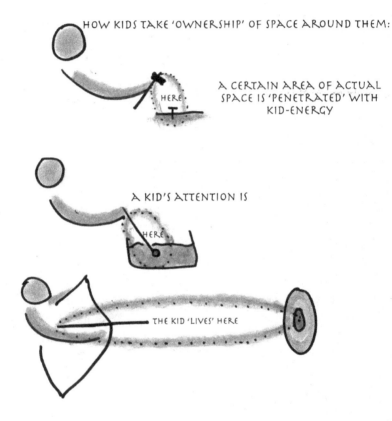

HOW KIDS TAKE 'OWNERSHIP' OF SPACE AROUND THEM:

A CERTAIN AREA OF ACTUAL
SPACE IS 'PENETRATED' WITH
KID-ENERGY

HERE

A KID'S ATTENTION IS

HERE

THE KID 'LIVES' HERE

KIDS NEED TO 'DIP' THEIR INVISIBLE 'WILL
TENTACLES' INTO THE PHYSICAL SURROUNDINGS TO
FIND THEIR POWERS.

WHEN THEY HAMMER A NAIL, STIR A POT OR HIT
A TARGET, A PART OF THEMSELVES HAS
CONNECTED TO THE OBJECT OF THEIR ATTENTION.

BY TRYING TO MASTER SOMETHING, THEY FILL THIS
ZONE WITH THEIR WILL AND THUS CONNECT WITH
IT.

Tenacity

Grit is not just a physical attribute. It is also psychological. That kind of invisible grit is often called tenacity. It, too, develops from overcoming things again and again. To be tenacious is to have the habit of overcoming difficulties socially and psychologically in a 'follow-though' way with whatever it may be.

Building Grit In Today's Kids

For kids today there are few places where grit can be developed. Kids are on the receiving end in today's world much longer than in prior times. Being a receiver is a more passive role and doesn't necessarily demand that much overcoming. All that is left for kids are buttons on machines do the rest. Grit-growth, as a result, was stolen from kids!

In fact, the more developed tools we have as a culture, the less grit-growth is possible for our children. Grit has to be a trait that parents are aiming at developing in their kids through sports or chores/care-giving. Developing grit in our children is panning out to be the same as developing real self-confidence, because kids get to know how strong will they have.

Small deeds like doing homework every day or brushing teeth every day all contribute to building will or some grit in this way. These habits of applying oneself cannot be built by the kid, alone. Either it has to be a harsh necessity from the environment that calls for this response again and again (five mile walk to school) or it is the parents/teachers that demand/expect it from the children. It has to be demanded again and again if grit should be developed in a person. For example, in the end the children might have both the psychological tenacity and physical muscle when they know how to walk, ski or run long distances.

Having built some grit gives children a great sense of accomplishment. That is because they truly have a sense that they can do a new thing well and for a long time. The grit-way has become a habit. When someone sees themselves doing some difficult deeds again and again and again, they gain a deep sense that they can do most anything! That is powerful.

All successful people all have grit, tenacity or stick-to-it-ness on various levels. These people, though, usually can admit that a person or a situation 'forced' them to pull themselves together and gain grit. Either life was tough or they had a person next to themselves steadying them all through childhood expecting a certain standard and not letting them off the hook. When a poor job was done, that person would tell the kid that they expected better than that. On behalf of the kid, they would *hold them to it.*

Summary of Chapter 16:

Since the machine age arrived, there are fewer physical areas where kids can develop will, stamina, or grit.

If kids are allowed an easy-street life, they may end up weak, anxious and with low self-esteem.

Having tough circumstances or demanding parents, can, in contrast, help kids to show their own mettle.

Real self-confidence will grow in such kids, since they already saw themselves do things. They know their own will and no one can take it from them.

BRUSHING DIRTY POTATOES FROM THE GARDEN GIVES A
KID FEEDBACK ON TWO THINGS:

1) DIRTY POTATOES ('THE WORLD')
2) THEIR OWN ABILITY TO CLEAN THEM (THEMSELVES)

A SCREEN ONLY GIVES FEEDBACK ON 'THE WORLD', NOT
ON THEMSELVES.

BRUSH, BRUSH

DOING THINGS IN THE REAL WORLD ASKS
SOMETHING FROM CHILDREN.
IT DEMANDS THAT THE CHILDREN ENTER AND
PERFORM ON THE STAGE OF LIFE SO THEY CAN FIND
THEMSELVES.

17. LESS REAL

Real And Unreal Kids

When a kid experiences the real world, a real kid will ensue. When a kid experiences a look-alike world, will they truly become real themselves? Can you say that you, yourself, are real when you are clueless of how reality works? We tell such people to 'get real'!

I will never forget the inner-city girl who finally dared to try milking my cow by hand. She still refused to believe that her 'brown' milk from the city had anything to do with this animal in front of us. A cool fridge with cartons of chocolate milk is a long ways away from this smelly animal that gave warm, white milk into the bucket.

This dirty reality of the barn could not connect with what she was used to at home. I don't blame her. We all have had experiences of kids believing in things that are a bit off or 'untrue'. An ad on TV may do some gimmick to be 'funny' but kids believe it at its face value. The cheese on a kid's pizza is a long way away from this animal, too. There aren't enough dots of first-hand experiences for most kids to manage to see the connections. The purpose of childhood is to get real. We often fail them here, because we forgot how it is to be a kid. And really, how could they know?

Unreal Experiences

We can with our technology make that getting-real journey longer for kids. Many toys give children false messages about how the world works. An example of this may be a play piano that churns out well-known tunes however you pound on it. What does that teach? In many ways we've created detours for learning how the world works with all our amusing contraptions. Was this just for selling something or grownups' amusement, we have to ask?

It is also poorly thought-through that we put our tots in front of a two-dimensional screen experience and think that they will figure out the other dimensions to life on their own. Did we think that the entirety of reality can came through the screen?

Only the two-dimensional surface of the world comes through a flat screen. We can, of course, make a 3-D movie happen in movie theaters and it is certainly a more powerful experience. But it is still unreal and make-believe. We are (momentarily) fooled as we live into the 'as if' experience of the movie. In fact, the content of these media are often manipulated to give us exaggerated our unreal experiences. We are given fake and fantastic attention-getting renderings instead of the truth.

We only have a chance to experience physical reality when it truly is actual physical reality we are in. But what if this screen time experience replaces the real and original one for many children so they hardly have time to experience real hard and fast reality?

Which reality is more real to them then? Isn't it clear that *where* we spend the most of our time obviously becomes most familiar and 'home-like' for us all? For 'professors' who live in their minds, that mind-world is more real. For bob-cat operators, the muck and earth they move with their machine is very real. For kids being on their phones or tablets, the same principle holds: whatever is going on *the most* in a kid's life is the *most* real.

WHEN WE ACT INTO OUR PHYSICAL ENVIRONMENT,
WE ERR.

FROM THE 'PAIN' THAT FOLLOWS, WE GET REAL AND LEARN
ABOUT OUR PLACE IN THE UNIVERSE.

Healthy and Unhealthy Fantasy

When kids play their games in physical reality they learn about physical laws *alongside* their imaginative play world. When they do chores, they learned about how physical reality works to an even tougher degree than in play. There is no time to 'invent' anything when washing the sinks in the bathroom. (It can take forever for a kid to clean the sink, but fooling around while doing a chore only makes the chore take longer to do, of course!)

Kids naturally want to live in a dreamy play world. What is different now with the screen is that fantasies are not self-created, but are instead, inserted into them. When kids are in the gaming world, they are dreaming the game makers' dreams in the daytime, not 'living' their own subconscious coming to the surface.

There are much fewer physical checks and balances when playing around on the tablet. The only thing that can physically break is their tablet. No branch can break or ball hit their heads. The kids may be physically 'safer' but they do not learn how to maneuver themselves more safely on the planet. As a result these kids are much more unsafe in the physical world than any previous generation ever was.

Adult Needs vs. Kid Needs

Our information age fits grownups' (unconscious) wish for more consciousness. A popular saying goes, "Think globally, but act locally." Thinking and traveling globally are activities that adults do more than children. We can be proud that we are advancing toward more global thinking compared to earlier times. But in industrialized countries, our local involvement has shrunk as we have moved to cities. This gives fewer reality checks for our kids with nature being so 'far away' from them.

Let's be clear: because of kids' newness on the earth, their biggest need is to find out what they can do and how they can fit in. Acting and exploring locally, therefore, were naturally always things kids did. They used the surroundings to poke and prod to find both themselves and the world.

The littler kids are, the more they should be allowed to be physically active into the surrounding environments. We forgot that kids always have played in a sandbox, the dirt or with the stones and sticks under their feet. We seem to think that kids aren't doing anything when they do those poke-jobs. But, really, they are learning of the hardness, wetness, coldness, stickiness of the earth. They are on their path to getting real with 'deeper learning' through their senses. This allows the kids to get *more* reality into themselves through their 'sense-communing' than any second-hand version of planet-life could ever provide.

Kids coming to us here are wanting experiences to connect to this place, not just knowledge or consciousness, yet. *First-hand experiences make them arrive here*, namely. From this point of view, both machines and technology do not answer kids' need to learn how this world truly works (with themselves included). Our inventions only put barriers between kids and this earth. We prevent our kids from connecting to everything around them.

In general, the electronic media's information-world (fake or true as it may be) robs our children of their need of connecting to the planet physically through *acting* locally. Only by being an actor ourselves does reality truly arrive for all of us.

Summary of Chapter 17:

We get real when we encounter real experiences. We get unreal when we are dealing with screen-content, and fantasy worlds.

When the large proportion of 'knowledge' for children are obtained from a screen, it takes longer for them to grasp reality.

Not 'getting real' can also be called being less mature. As a consequence of technology, our kids mature slower.

VIRTUAL REALITY

OUR HEADS CAN MAKE THE MISTAKE OF THINKING
THAT ITS OWN MENTAL WORLD IS ALL IT NEEDS.

THAT MISTAKE CAN BE FATAL!

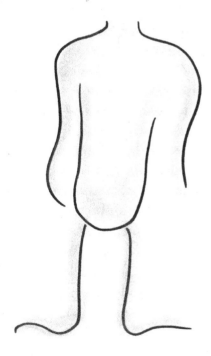

18. LESS FINDING OF THEMSELVES

Finding Ourselves Outside Of Ourselves

When a kid is digging a hole in the sand in an old fashioned sandbox, they forget themselves in the doing of it; dig, dig, dig. Afterwards they can see how their power and will affected the outer world. A hole in the sand is visible.

Concrete situations in the real world are necessary for kids to get real and awake. For kids, it happens in this order: First we forget ourselves as we are engrossed in, for example, the digging of the hole. Our will activity unfolds. Then we wake up to our own power as we look at the hole we dug after the fact. It is a stark consciousness-contrast; we *forget ourselves* when doing the physical deed and then consciously *realize ourselves* when looking at what we did.

This is how kids wake up to their own power that comes, after all, out of themselves. What came out of themselves equals something of themselves, obviously. What I did must be some part of ME.

The truth is that none of us would truly believe in our own capabilities unless we had seen the outcomes of these capabilities.

Kids Need To Relate

To find themselves as a reality, kids need to relate to things in a small and very personal way, *in reality*. They have to *give themselves over* to the thing experienced. They have to see that they themselves matter for the world. They, simply, have to *mean something* for other creatures and people.

Kids find themselves through relationships that are, in a small way, personally meaningful because there was a real response (from both themselves and the environment) that made them find purpose at the other end of their own interacting. This other end is a person or a concrete thing that they now have connected to. It is often dubious what is really at the other end when we are on 'the virtual'.

Not Finding Ourselves

When childhoods are spent in front of computer screens, children do not see themselves making hard-and-fast imprints anywhere. They perform deeds in the virtual landscape that are stored on "clouds," but the prints they make on the virtual mental world are mostly neither concrete nor personal. They know deep-down that it just as well could have been another kid and no one real would have noticed a difference.

Because of this fact, it is less possible for them to experience their own individuality on an electronic device, compared to in the three-dimensional world of nature and real humans. That is, as mentioned before, partly due to the virtual landscape giving them a softer, less individualized and mostly preprogrammed feedback, as compared to the immediate and coarse physical world around them. The physical body's interactions with physical reality here on the ground can literally ground a person. But conversely, interacting with fantasy-filled screens entails connecting with non-concrete, cloud-like things, fantasy things.

It is not possible to have the same experience digging in a sandbox of the real world as one would have in the virtual world of a flat screen. The power in oneself that is found by winning in a computer game is the power of mental concentration, mostly. That is a totally *different power* than the one that emerged by digging a hole in the earth's surface.

We have made a world where our machines and screens alike have taken away kids' need to do that much stuff themselves. Children do not need to get into it anymore, not outside in their backyards, not alone or together with others. This makes their life seem less dirty and less dangerous but certainly less alive. When we let children live on the reflected light's screens in large doses, we didn't think about the most serious consequence of all:

The fact that children do not develop an adequate sense of themselves.

When a kid doesn't try out things of this world, like climbing a tree or wandering through a woods or planting something in the dirt, we are teaching a three-fold negative lesson to our kid. We are inadvertently telling them that

1) they are not capable to deal with the concrete, and
2) the earth has nothing to teach (and isn't worth loving), and
3) the physical world out there is too dangerous and hard.

Healthy Experiencing

A healthy dynamic for letting your kid find out about themselves goes like this:

1. You must allow them exposure to the actual physical and social situation.
2. As you are giving/allowing that exposure, *your belief in your kid* that they can handle it needs to be there accompanying the event.
3. As your kid's responses come out, you must steady them with your response (praise/scold them).

The most important ingredient is the fact that the kid's responses to the situation can find an outlet and that the 'world's' response to the kids' effort also can take place. The child acted and the 'world' re-acted. Or the 'world' acts and the child re-acts. This 'tango' of the child touching the real world and the world touching the child is how kids get to know themselves.

As this tango takes place, children's responses come out of themselves in mysterious ways that they had no idea about. How can a child find out that they are a more 'pastel' person unless they compare their paintings to their peers who prefer bold colors? How can you know that you are good at cleaning all the crumbs off the counter top, unless you saw yourself be praised for making it nice in the kitchen?

How can a child know that they are good at bicycling, unless they and you saw them cycling along with ease? The flavors of who they are emerge with every activity they perform. Being then received and seen for having those attributes helps the child solidify their sense of themselves. Thus their self confidence grows with every action performed in this world.

The problem is therefore in today's tablet world that so many basic planetary experiences have been hijacked by our machines. The normal human responses to these basic experiences on many subtle levels have now been omitted for the technological child.

A kid in Mongolia carrying water buckets from the river on the winter snow will get a certain self-knowledge that a tablet kid will miss. Our kid, instead, sits with an i-phone in their hands, and does a pre-programmed 'about-the-world' bit of learning or amusement that doesn't teach them anything about themselves. They are an onlooker to the world and they really don't matter much. We protected them from hardships, but stole their opportunities to see what they were made of and able to do. We have made most of our technological kids obsolete for their surroundings, more or less. Most of them do not contribute to anything but their own amusement 'inside' their devices.

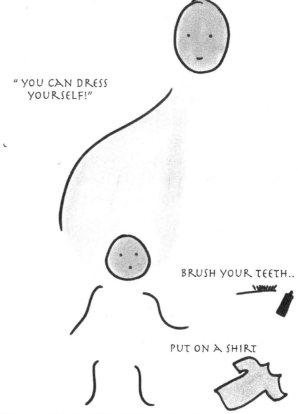

" YOU CAN DRESS YOURSELF!"

BRUSH YOUR TEETH..

PUT ON A SHIRT

JUST AS WORK HABITS HAVE TO BE INSTILLED, SO ALSO DOES THE SENSE OF BEING RESPONSIBLE FOR SOMETHING.

WE FIRST LEARN TO BE RESPONSIBLE FOR OURSELVES. THE NEXT STEP IS BECOMING RESPONSIBLE FOR OTHER THINGS BESIDES OURSELVES. THAT ALSO HAS TO BE INSTILLED!

Summary of Chapter 18:

Children learn primarily by relating personally to things in a concrete way. This 'tangible' learning takes place before they relate to the same topic in an abstract and truthful mind-way.

This 'tangible' learning means that their own senses have to be used in a touching and feeling way before abstract activity in their minds can arise in a healthy way.

When kids are interacting in the physical world, they forget themselves in the will-response that emanates from their own little person.

We adults have forgotten how precious those personal response-activities are for kids. Through seeing their will come from themselves, our children get to know themselves on a deep level!

Children cannot learn about what they, themselves, are by being onlookers. They have to immerse themselves in the concrete reality, physically and socially. They have to be left to deal with some piece of this world to see what comes out of themselves to meet it!

Where children are busily active is where they actually experience themselves and develop the capacities that are needed for their future.

Each time a child responds appropriately to their surroundings, they find themselves connecting and belonging to this world.

GETTING TO KNOW MYSELF WILL NOT HAPPEN
UNLESS I GET INVOLVED

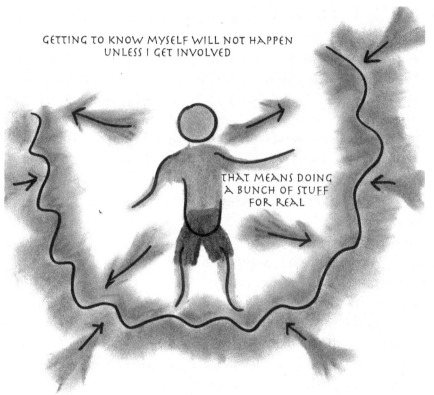

THAT MEANS DOING
A BUNCH OF STUFF
FOR REAL

BEING A HUMAN IN A BODY IS REALLY DEALING WITH A
CONGLOMERATE OF VARIOUS 'FORCES' THAT I NEED TO
FIGURE OUT.
PLANET EARTH IS A PERFECT PLACE FOR SEEING THOSE
'FORCES' IN ACTION.

THE PARADOXICAL FACT IS THAT AS I EXPLORE
EVERYTHING IN SPACE AROUND ME, I ALSO LEARN HOW
I, MYSELF, WORK.

THUS THE BY-PRODUCT OF EXPERIENCING THE CONCRETE
WORLD IS 'FINDING MYSELF'!

Conclusions from the Second Section

If the arguments in this section ring true, the consequence for parents and teachers must be the admission that the way our society thinks about children and guides their childhoods must change.

In a nutshell, these admissions are:

- We grownups cannot 'teach' the full reality of things to kids.
- Reality has to be experienced directly to sink in all the way.

Furthermore, the problems with too much technology for modern children are two-fold:

- Kids that are over-exposed to technology will not know the real world.
- These kids will also end up not knowing who they, themselves, are.

Section 3

MAKING A MORE
BALANCED FUTURE

In this section we illustrate how you, the parent, can take the power back that our high-tech society has seemingly removed from you. It is your right to give the form and content to your children's childhoods that they need, and it is critical for your children that you do so!

We will start by outlining how you can effectively do that in the context of the challenges that face you and your child with school, peer-pressure, unwanted influences, other authorities, etc. It is not easy to be a parent these days. Good parenting means taking charge, making judgments, setting boundaries, trusting gut feelings, being a good example, and balancing out hangups.

We will address developing the 'human thing' in our kids in the face of a world immersed in technology and mechanistic, input-output thinking that is foreign to what kids are, biologically and spiritually. We will attempt to define what it means to be a bottom-line human being, followed by sketching out principles and ways and guidelines for ensuring that kids turn out to be real human beings amidst our technological jungle by fostering life-bringing activities.

We will delve into more insight into how kids function and how parents and educators can enable our children to be able to live and fulfill their lives, their _own_ lives, not some kind of generic life! Our children will need to develop inward mobility, attentiveness, and capacities for managing the varied tasks that life will challenge them with if they are to best unfold their individualized life story with themselves as captains.

Children learn and acquire habits in accordance with the expectations of their parents and the surrounding, educational culture. The last section of this book gives parents and guardians some pointers on what habits to focus on for raising a child that is life competent, not just a virtual wiz.

19. PARENTS, TAKE POWER!

"WHEN SHOULD I SAY 'NO' TO MY KID?"

"WHAT KIND OF
FOOD SHOULD
THEY EAT?
WHEN IS BED -
TIME?"

IF YOU, THE PARENT, WON'T CHOOSE, THE 'WORLD'
WILL CHOOSE FOR YOU.
YES, IT IS YOUR TURN TO DECIDE WHAT IS BEST FOR
YOUR KID! YOUR JUDGEMENT WILL DO. NOT THE KIDS',
SINCE THEY DO NOT HAVE THE ABILITY TO JUDGE YET.

In today's world, parents have different responsibilities than before because human communities and the social fabric within the family have changed. When society isn't in agreement about what is right or wrong, things are harder for kids. Therefore, it is also clearly more challenging for parents, too.

Though parenting requires outwardly more flexibility than ever, inwardly parents have to be more of the rock onto which their child needs to hold. You, the guardian, need to know that you are much more important than school and after-school activities. You are much more important than friends who come in and out of your child's life. You are the ground on which your child stands. You have more power than before and, as a result, more responsibility for what values are taught in our chaotic world. Therefore, it is critical that we understand our children and our own role as we are guiding and educating them.

Here are a few things to remember:

Childhood is a time to mature. The education of children has to do with their gradual maturation as humans. A wise old sage can feel for everything around him and can understand the connections between many things in life. He has the possibility to be objective in his empathy. But a little child is still exploring and being "young and foolish" and subjective about everything.

The kid feels the emotions of those around him too, but in an unfree, self-immersed way. Kids may cry when another kid cries, but their empathy is partly for their *own* sadness caused by the other kid's sadness. That's just how it is. Growing old is about gaining distance from things inwardly, but that doesn't mean with less empathy! This is the gradual maturation process that humans go through. We could say that aging means freeing ourselves, bit by bit, from the emotional oceans that we were swimming in when we were younger.

Our job as educators is to guide and frame the young-and-foolish exploration phase our kids go through. By participating in life's various processes, trying out a few things, and even being allowed to make a bunch of mistakes, children develop a realistic view of themselves amidst the world that is around them. This real world will *naturally* mature kids and make them more objective about themselves as they gain experience upon experience. The virtual world, in contrast, may not do that.

New Hidden Internet Dangers

Despite all the programs available to parents for controlling what children watch on the internet, many parents don't know what their kids are doing on-line. However, the virtual landscapes are full of new and unforeseen dangers for kids and adults. Though it is accepted that we need to make our kids safe from physical dangers, the new psychological dangers in the on-line culture are unchartered territories whose impact on kids is not fully fathomed.

The ideals of youth in today's on-line world are to a large extent steered by the self-interest of commerce. Advertisements and sensationalism are, from this point of view, the new snakes in childhood's paradise.

Media-influenced ideals of coolness subconsciously define how kids need to be, act, and look so they can survive in school and not be left out. When this on-line influence replaces kids' own inner life and mental image-making, our children's minds get co-opted. Their minds get shaped by the commercial industries inserting wants and urges into them. We cannot call this anything else but an insidious and under-the-radar indoctrination process.

In a parallel way, our democracy is influenced by campaign ads from politicians with the most money. Results would not be so skewed if all of us were thinking critically on our own. The more often some slogan is said, the more swayed we seem to be, however untruthful it is!

As parents, we should be aware that the ads as well as the consumer culture, in general, are actively trying to 'diminish' your child unless they buy, buy, buy. Many parents fight with their kids over the high prices of the cool clothing.

Of course, parents also realize how painful it is to not fit into a 'tribe' at school, and therefore they often end up letting the kids look like everyone else, despite the price tag. We all have to make necessary compromises. Pressure from school 'culture' wins a little and our home values win a little. If we do not make some compromises, at times, we may create a vacuum where kids end up doing devious things behind our backs. We parents, after all, were responsible for putting our kids into the school-value-complex. We need to endorse it to a certain degree or our child's world turns out to become schizophrenic.

Your job as parent is to be conscious of all those places of hidden influence that are preying on your children—media, friends, you name it—to the best of your ability. If you are not sure something is a good thing for your child, you are allowed to probe and find out more information about it. *You ultimately decide*, not the peer pressure from friends!

School

School is not an ideal place to get to know oneself on a deeper level except for within academic pursuits. Because kids have a *subconscious quest to find out their own power*, they *must* pursue that quest amidst taking classes. They must figure out who they are in relationship to everyone and everything in the setting they are in. Being in school with peers of the same age, ends up providing opportunities for finding-out about oneself in the context of coolness and popularity.

Later in life, our children will see through this game and their reality will build on real and honest relationships, not on who is cooler at the work place. If we remain stuck in a 'wannabe', popularity-seeking state, we end up being seen as immature when we are an adult.

School is therefore not good preparation grounds for actual social skills in life itself. Efforts to increase popularity or perceived status through social climbing unfold when people do not know each other very well. Thus a kid's 'role-play' in school settings may seem somewhat fake later on in their work life where the bottom line is that everyone needs to be seen for who they are and what they can do.

School can be seen as an artificial storage place where certain (animal) herd behaviors can be learned. All that can be developed in this impersonal setting is a pecking-order-system. The reason why popularity-ranking occurs is the homogeneous groups we put kids in. When everyone is very similar, ranking oneself is the only way to 'find oneself' within the class or 'herd' of similar-aged people.

Kids need to figure out their own power socially, practically and intellectually. They have no other way to pursue this knowledge quest except by comparing themselves to their peers in their school setting. School, as we know it, provides few practical tasks in which kids can realize their own power. Shop classes are mostly gone.

The less a kid finds himself intellectually in school, the more he needs to find himself somewhere else. Besides the class subjects, the only thing that is available is *other* kids. Kids have an unconscious drive to become the most they can become. Therefore, they cannot *but* strive to become more popular or at least be seen as a trouble maker!

All kids have a driven 'duty' to *take* the power they can, *where* and *when* they can, whether on the sports field or in the context of status amongst peers. Taking power for oneself is the same as what animals do when they are marking territories and struggling for social position. It is not the specifically human 'thing'. It has to do more with survival than our higher human principles! 'Peeing on posts' or marking of territory or turf is probably the reptile brain speaking. Ranking for status is the mammalian brain expressing itself.

These two 'lower' brains have a positive role by ruling in the animal world and are there for the purpose of ordering nature. Having a bull in the field will protect the herd. But having a bully in the school grounds leads most of the other kids to feel like underlings. If this herd-ranking continues into adult society, we have a totalitarian regime or a tyrannical boss. Humans aren't happy under such conditions. We like it better when we are all valued and can have a say, without a bullying dictator telling us what to do or not to do.

Socially, humans are happiest when everyone is included in a more democratic way. That social ideal is hard to achieve in our schools. That is not because the teachers and some mature kids aren't trying hard to make it a good place. It is because the large class sizes and the homogeneity of the groupings lend themselves to ranking and pecking orders, just like in the military.

Being Cool

If your kid is of the few that are cool in the context of the school setting, he can gain the idea that he is really more important than the average kid. Most kids feel not-so-cool while in large settings, since there is room for only one 'leader' or 'queen-bee' in a herd. Being popular and cool is not necessarily the same as practicing being a true leader, and it can inhibit other, lower status kids from taking leadership roles. The fact is that all kids will have to become leaders of their own and others' lives, and they should begin practicing being leaders in school!

Unfortunately, while they are in school, most kids experience the herd-reality: that they are mostly small, insignificant and unseen entities that don't matter. But since kids so desperately want to be seen by grownups and kids alike, they try, in an unfree way, to rise to the top *where they can be seen* better. That place is reserved for the most popular kid in school.

Many parents hope or believe that their kid is fairly popular. But is that cool place a position where a kid is seen for *who they really are*? Seriously, do you think that being cool is a good role to have to play? A cool kid is not one who shows his feelings. A cool kid is a generic-beauty that can be a herd-ideal or prom queen or king.

A cool kid can very seldom be an interesting 'character' such as an individualized kid who does inventive things that are out of the norm. Those 'character' kids are more often in the un-cool theater department. Most of those kids have let go of the ideal of being popular. Such theater kids try out all kinds of roles. They are on a roll to figure themselves out as they relate to each acting part they are allowed to play. In contrast, the cool kid only has the possibility to play one role: A generic cool kid.

Personally, I have often wished for the coolest kid to play a non-type-cast part in the school play! That would actually free him or her from the glorious but nevertheless fixed position of being so cool! Giving an education is, after all, about preparing a kid, in the best way, for life itself. Seldom will a cool kid continue being cool after graduating from school. That was only a situational opportunity. As one mom said so well, "I don't want my kid to be cool! I actually want my kid to be *warm*!" How about that?

As a parent you need to counteract the popularity game that happens at school. If you don't, your child can become stuck for life with the role they learned to play in school. Remember that life, in its progression, will ask them to play many different kinds of roles. These roles need practicing, if life isn't going to be too hard. For this reason you have to give your child different opportunities for role-play including powerful leadership roles and humble servant roles and on and on. Look for those settings where such role-play is possible. You will find more of these places away from school.

Unwanted Influences

It can be very difficult to be responsible for our kid's universe as they spend more time than ever away from their family's oversight. In the past, parents had more actual hours in the day to influence a child. Nowadays, a few minutes in the car on the way to school or activities is often all you get.

Parenting becomes increasingly more difficult when other parents are parenting less. Other grownups have different ideas about what is right or wrong for children. You intuitively know that you have to find families with similar values to your own. When you find these people, please realize how precious they are. They can become your new extended 'family'.

You are in charge of excluding a lot of the media onslaught on our kids in today's world. The littler our kids are, the more we protect them, of course. Later, when your kids are older, you can talk to them about what images were disturbing. Big kids can free themselves from the shocking images more easily than little kids can.

Believe in your own judgment about what influences you want to expose your kid to. You have an evolving sense of which culture you would prefer for your kid to absorb. At the same time, wherever you put your children, you have a duty to uphold your decision to put them there until you can realistically change course and find a better solution.

Upholding Authorities in Their Places

It the last decades, the importance for kids to grow up in a coherent world has become increasingly clear. Coherency means that the adults in the community surrounding the children more or less agree on what is good and what is bad. This coherent world view, we remember, is what was called the 'village' or academically speaking: an *authoritative* community. You, the parents, are now in charge of making your kids' world as coherent and whole as possible.

If school is in line with your own values, it will clearly benefit your child more than if it isn't. If you speak respectfully about the other adults in your kid's milieu, it will be a good thing for your kids. If you speak critically about other adults that your children will have to obey, your children will be harmed by it.

Your child cannot but absorb and reflect your judgments on everything and everyone. Kids have no choice. *You* do have the choice, in how you want to portray and respect other adults. Kids, in contrast, are made to follow the parents' emotional judgments of good and bad, whether they want to or not. That is because children cannot but lean into and align themselves with everything around them, with you as their guiding light.

A child's world cracks if they have to live within two opposing value systems with one of their parents being negative towards the other one. On the other hand, it is great that kids can so readily accept that different places can have different rules! Without losing away your own authority at home, you can tell your kids to do what other grownups want them to do while in their places.

Kids feel safer in a world where there is mutual respect for those adults who are the 'holders' of a place's value system. Thus, they will be open, love, and *learn a lot* from a person whom they sense their parents respect. Intuitively, children like the idea that they, too, will be respected when they are older. It is a tragedy when children cannot look up to someone! This is especially the case in the grade-school years.

We need to learn to empower our kids to receive from others in this way. When we don't allow this, it is because we are actually more occupied with *ourselves and our own process* in figuring out what _we_ believe in, rather than being taken up with our kids' well being.

Being a parent means that we are in charge. But because we have developed a more objective position than our kids, the kids' best comes first! Your kids' best is to live in a whole, un-cracked universe with grownups supporting each other. If others undermine you as a parent, you, of course, cannot tango with them, either! For your child's best, you should always look for the least broken world for your child.

For this reason, when you put your child in a school, or at grandma's home, or with your ex-spouse, you must support it as a good influence for your child. Don't undermine it. Tell your child to listen and do as the adults say when they are there. Be open to the fact that there may be good things there that you haven't grasped as of yet. We know that transition times for value systems are hard for the kids. Try to have those be as predictable as possible, for your kids' sake. Longer stretches in each place are therefore also easier on the kids than frequent back and forth stays.

In short: you are in charge of teaching your own value system to your children but you are also in charge of teaching respect for others. You are teaching two things, your own culture and value system alongside tolerance for other's culture, choices, and views. You cannot do both unless you have developed a certain distance within yourself toward your own choices. That inward objectivity comes gradually for all of us, of course. Let's give each other a break as far as that parental maturation process goes, since neither children nor grownups can mature on command!

The Judgment-Call of a Parent is Everything

Since we parents are in the process of discovering our own values while we parent, it can be pretty hard to not be reactive rather than mature and supportive of folks with opposing values to our own. It is, for sure, a balancing act.

It takes being strong to build strong family traditions and rules in our own home when the traditions are not like everyone else's. Whether Julia gets to do social media in her room at night is *our* decision. It is *our* call whether in it is more important for Johnny to be social with the group of boys and see that movie with them or if he should stay home. Judgment call after judgment call—*that* is what parenting is all about.

But we parents *must* take charge, we *must* judge. It is our turn now to autonomously make decisions. This was not so in earlier times when the tribal leader and survival issues were right in parents' faces.

The main thing in today's parenting is to remember that your calm and grounded judgment call is the most important ingredient in your children's lives, however you twist and turn it. The use of your inner weighing power—your higher self in gear—is given to you as you play 'the little god' in your kid's universe. Everything hinges on it. ***Do it.***

Not having any opinions or steadfastness would teach our kids to be leaves in the wind. That is not a safe place to be. We serve them best by working on *being sure* of what we choose and by standing by our decisions and enforcing family 'law'. The more self-assured we are, the more we model that self-confidence for our kids and build their sense of security and feeling of empowerment. Of course, we must also constantly learn about new views and ideas ourselves so we can become surer in our decision-making.

Setting Boundaries, Breaking Boundaries

Boundaries are products of our judgment activity. When we set a bed time, it was because we had seen that the kids didn't thrive after a certain hour. To give our children the right boundaries requires that we really see and hear our kids as they develop. They, by going through a natural maturing process, have new needs all the time. If we do not see them accurately, we are in danger of 'abusing' them in a passive way by enforcing out-dated boundaries. For example, putting most five-year-olds in a crib would be outdated!

You, as a parent or teacher, are the captain of your ship. Though staying the course can be a good thing for stability, we need to have inward mobility and sound judgment to deal with new dangers in the waters ahead. It is an intelligent captain's prerogative to change course for the good of their brood.

Kids *totally accept* that you may change course if your judgment informs you to do so!

Your grounded judgment based on your senses will guide you in your boundary setting. Look at your kid, listen to him, feel his paleness or rosy cheeks. Is she happy? Is she content? Is he stressed? Is he feeling inadequate? Should the kid have 'down time'? Look at your kids and ask yourself if they seem secure and brave and encouraged. Ask yourselves what is needed to balance your kids' day. You probably are doing this intuitively anyway.

In addition to setting boundaries to keep *too much* of the 'world' out of your kid's life, you may conversely have to deal with fearful behavior in kids that stops them from participating in life. In this case, you need to help the child to break loose from his or her fears and self-imposed boundaries.

If you never went in the woods as a kid, you may never feel comfortable in the woods later in life. Kids may develop neuroses if we don't expose them to natural things. So-called *exposure therapy* can smooth out these hang-ups. When kids are afraid of dogs, simply go often to a house with a dog! In contrast, if the child is too unafraid of dogs, you will need to stop them from racing towards the animal. Their impulses need to be curbed to have them remain safe. You create a mini-pain by scolding them to protect them from the maxi-pain that a dog bite would inflict. You are all the time the judge of what is worth being worried about for real and, in the same go, you must smooth out made-up fears.

The art of parenting is to steady the child so they can become a confident, but not over-confident, doer. You want your child to feel mastery over things, so have them *finish* tasks! They can then get the satisfaction of seeing their deeds on the outside of themselves. This makes them feel competent.

You are the one who shows the child what is worth being afraid of or not. If the child is afraid of something that isn't worth the worry, you must show the unafraid action (even though your child may be resisting). We have to make our kids feel that we, not their fears, are in charge. How can *they* possibly know what is dangerous?

Parents must give kids loving but true mini-lessons of life itself. We are the intermediary and softener of the harsh world out there. Sometimes that requires us to be tougher and more unrelenting (like the big world would be) and other times we need to sympathize with our child. Parenting is not about ourselves being who *we* want to be. It is about what lessons our kids need to learn.

Take Charge!

Often, parents do not take up the critical role of being the primary people belonging to and influencing their own kids. Many parents truly aren't sure they have the authority to fill that power-position. They may put their kid on medications instead of daring to put their kid in his place.

These parents also may not dare to take on the unpopular role of drawing kids out of their virtual social lives or video games. Many parents 'suffer' when their kids whine and complain but they do not dare to do anything to change it. They do not trust their own judgment as to what a content and happy kid looks like.

Start trusting your gut feelings! Letting kids be where they want to be, instead of gripping into their lives, is shirking your job as a parent or guardian. A guardian is supposed to guard their charge! By not 'pushing and pulling' on the kids, you are neglecting them to their own devices, literally! This can lead to isolation for your child. It can also lead to being in a social world with peers who do not know right from wrong. You know that better than they!

Social media addiction and video game addiction have become big problems. If parents had noticed and had the courage to take charge at a much earlier stage, their children wouldn't have progressed down these anti-social lanes. We parents are asked to be stronger than ever because we must resist the peer pressure from other parents who are not taking charge.

I reiterate, the sometimes unpleasant task of taking charge of your kid's life is *not* about you. It is about your kid and what is best for him or her.

Being the Master of Ourselves as Parents

Grownups have higher selves that enable them to pull themselves up by their 'bootstraps'! Kids don't have this ability to overcome themselves, yet. A kid cannot do the hard thing first, unless we help them to do so.

Our specific human thing is that our bodies can do something animals cannot. We have the ability to learn to overcome ourselves and do what is hard and right, despite our lusts and urges. For animals, surviving on the planet is dictated by obeying strong urges and instincts. But for humans, our higher self must tell our lower self what to do or not do.

Learning to overcome ourselves does not feel natural. It's work, and it can be painful. It always had to be forced upon us from the outside by social rules. These outer pressures may be missing in our technological world. That is a problem.

If everybody eats their TV dinner in their rooms, table manners will not be instilled. If outer pressures pushing, pulling, drawing, and forming the kid aren't working on the child from the outside in, to instill manners and good habits, their brains will naturally not get the indentations needed for 'holding back' urges and overcoming natural desires.

Adults are supposed to have gained the ability to control themselves and to delay gratification. If this objective distance between our desires and our higher selves does not develop, we remain immature children inside.

The transformation of being ruled by the outside world into being ruled by our own inner, higher principles, based on sensing right from wrong, hasn't happened in an immature adult. Instead, peer pressures and sensory stimuli rule by necessity unless there are cultural imperatives, like the rules of a religious group, helping people to behave.

The bringing up of children entails that parents play the role of being their higher selves *for* them. The guardians are the 'substitute' until the children can carry this 'judgment capacity' within themselves. It usually takes until we are around twenty-one years old.

Because children are more fused with their desires and their environments through their senses, it is necessary that the adult guardians play the higher-self role until the children can master their own horses.

By being a fully responsible parent, you prepare the child's daily activities to become *useful habits* to have for their later life. These habits of learning to "wait!", "help out with chores", "be polite!" are your gifts towards your children's future. When the kids have acquired the habits of delaying gratification in childhood, holding their urges will be easier as an adult. If *we* do not impose ourselves *on them* by expecting this and that *from them*, they will need to create good habits later on in their own lives, if they can.

Because your job as a parent is to give the kids good habits, it is critical to fully take charge of them. This is where a robot-parent wouldn't do! A kid and their actions need to be identified and seen by a real human who corrects their behaviors. A child needs to be 'caught' when doing inappropriate deeds, or even when they are having inappropriate feelings and thoughts. They also, of course, need to be praised when they are doing the right things. How else can they know how to relate appropriately?

Kids Swim in the 'Waters' of our Attitudes

Little children copy the actions and emotional framework of their parents and other caretakers. They manifest who we are inwardly as people in their interactions at school and with other children. They manifest our vision of life. This means that we are responsible for their outlook.

If we want our children to be kind, it means that we must model kindness. If we want our children to be fair, that means we must model fairness. They will pick up who we really are, warts and all. Our actions as well as attitudes will carry our children by example. If we model the attitude that we *together can make* a beautiful world of compassionate and generous folks, they will too. In a similar manner, kids also (helplessly) imbibe our open or close-mindedness, and our trust or distrust in people.

By taking charge of them you model how a person should live. That is the most important ingredient in your kids' lives, since leading their own lives is what they are inadvertently hoping to do themselves. You will want to show them how you join the good things and the good people of the world, and not show them fear for everything and everybody. First, model what you want a human being to be; second, expect the same from your child.

Kids accept that we, too, learn from our mistakes. Do not think that you are a perfect parent. That parent does not exist! Your humble and truthful attitude will be modeled, too! It is o.k. to admit mistakes. You are just then making it easier for your child to admit their mistake next time something goes wrong.

Despite misadventures, you may be surprised to find that your children easily and happily follow you on your next adventure without blinking an eye. But that is how kids are made: to take you fully as their captain. New direction? No problem!

Summary of Chapter 19

Whether you want to or not, you as parent are the 'ruler' and the ground on which your kid walks. You must fearlessly take on your role in order to do right by your kid. Your firm and calm judgments are building blocks for your child's own self confidence later.

You can help kids navigate the dangers of the internet, peer pressure, the cool game and social ranking games in school. It is important that you help balance the kids with the right experiences to break up fearful hangups. In addition to this, you alone hold the reigns to empower other grownups to be positive influences for your children.

As a parent you model what it means to be a human being for your children, so, model well! But give yourself a break as far as making 'mistakes'. <u>Children are created to be able to accept that you change course when necessary.</u>

Don't be afraid to make judgment calls, enforce family law, and set boundaries. But be able to change directions and boundaries as conditions change.

20. DEVELOPING THE
HUMAN 'THING'

Our Tools are Our 'Brain Children'

All of our tools, from shovels to computers, are our culture's 'brain children'. The thinking that went into our machines express the clever and awake observation of phenomena, the mental ability to deduct cause and effect from them, and the determination to apply them to solving physical problems. Humanity has applied the laws of physics with this kind of logical thinking. All tools show that cause and effect processes in our physical world have been totally mastered and understood. Engineers internalized a work problem, and voila, the tool in front of us can solve it better than our hands can by themselves.

Are our tools the pinnacle of human development? Because we now are inundated with high-tech gadgets and machines, we can tend to think that this is the best and most advanced part of ourselves! But, is logical cause and effect thinking actually the highest aspect of being human? Even though we know that humans hatched the ideas that produced these tools, they express only one aspect of our humanness. We are much more than our deductive type of thinking!

In contrast to machines, living organisms have *different* laws infusing them. Take, for example, a blue flower growing out of a tiny, gray seed. We could never have predicted that the flower would be blue from that particular gray seed of this particular plant if we had not seen it before, say in last year's flower garden.

Plants, like all living bodies, do a development-thing to which we only can only marvel in awe. We did not make that progression happen and we have not figured out how to make something big, blue, and beautiful come out of something small, grey, and seemingly insignificant. We can completely understand a machine, but a living organism is far harder to understand, even though scientists try.

As much as we try to make a living organism, we have to admit that we are only beginning to scratch the surface of what life, itself, really is. Babies that come out of our bodies arrive because of our own bodies' wisdom, not because we consciously made them.

Being part of the natural world ourselves, we have both mechanical and living principles inside ourselves. In addition to the machine-like, cause-and-effect aspect of our own bodies that we especially can see in our bone structures, we also embody the mysterious transformational aspect that plants show us. Just as when we look at the little grey seed and do not know exactly how it will grow, we do not know how and why our children will want to express their lives when they are fully grown.

We rightfully should show awe and respect for what our children will strive to become: We wish them to truly express themselves, not something that we determined on their behalf. Imagine if our own parents had decided who *we* became!

Children carry secrets of change and metamorphosis that cannot be predicted by those of us who raise them. We guardians can, maybe, sense some unfathomable dimensions behind the new human being in front of us. We don't know where they come from or why they go through the surprising metamorphoses that they go through as they mature. This dynamic aspect of humans makes us participants in the mystery of Life. Life's middle names are change, evolution, development, and metamorphosis, not fixed cause and effect in a mechanical sense.

Machine Thinking About Kids

Because we live in an age dominated by machines and computer technology, we tend to think in machine analogies. This is because we are surrounded by small and large machines that are 'brain children' of input-output thinking. Unconsciously, we think that humans are born like new, unused computers; blank slates that need filling up by our education systems. We even use the term 'download' for educating ourselves!

We tend to think of children as empty receivers of our curricula. We do not focus on how the children can transform *our* factoids into something that is meaningful for *their* actual life. We don't focus on that life-incorporating aspect of children that comes forth out of their selves.

On the whole, we are more focused on our own curriculum and on how well the kids test on it. This is a mechanical input-output expectation from our children. We are not asking them to add or create anything new. This is clearly because we do not believe that the kids have anything to contribute. While they may not have much to contribute to the body of knowledge about Henry the Eighth, for example, a child would be able to 'digest' *for themselves* more if they could_*do* something with the stories they hear. That could be having the kids make a drawing, or writing an essay, or acting the king's role in a play.

Reciting back textbook content in a test does not cultivate the *living part* of a kid that tries to make organic meaning of the body of learning for their very own life. If the child can work through the topic themselves, especially in an artistic way, the content will be more meaningful for them. This is because their own life-creative-energy has become involved, not just their cognitive selves.

Most school curricula don't consider what comes forward from each human being as they make the effort to 'grasp' both mental and practical topics. In this book, we referred earlier to some invisible 'tentacle' that is doing this 'grasping'. What we refer to is the individual child's living, invisible will.

The will, invisible as it is in its nature, comes out of us and touches and reaches for things. The effect or the print of our will become visible only after a deed is accomplished. This will or invisible 'tentacle' emerges from deep down within ourselves. If we have no need to develop will and grit when we are children, we will not exercise and develop practical will capacities. Modern technological children do not have well developed, invisible, practical will 'tentacles' or 'roots' in their environments. Their wills are probably less developed than those of royal princes of the past!

Humans vs. Machines

A machine does not have its own will in the same way a human does. A machine is there to better and more effectively execute human will impulses. We have made them to be our new 'slaves' or servants. They vacuum up the dust from the floor, wash and dry our clothes, run errands on the computer via Amazon, and so on.

The role of being a servant is the rightful place of a machine! If the machines take over the world, we have reason to worry. And we do worry about that because machine thinking tends to rule some areas of our life now.

Nevertheless, we insist that we have more heart than does a robot. We prefer to see ourselves as being more flexible than a machine in how we do things. We like to think that we are not machine-like and preprogrammed by our schools, that we have more inspiration and creativity than a computer can have. We'd like to believe that we have something inside us that has to do with free experience, not just a preprogrammed dictate for each of our activities.

Deep down, we do not want to become a robot!

Having a heart, being flexible, and getting inspired are qualities that machines cannot have, we hope. These are all capacities of movement, "un-stuckness," that are human possibilities connected to being alive. Unlike machines that are more or less fixed on a task, we can grow and change. We can be creative like the gods with our godlike spark within. This spark which is the core of what we are, our 'I am!', can be touched by the muses and be inspired. That has been the experience of humans through the ages. Why shouldn't that be the experience of our children, too?

Our scary sci-fi movies try to warn us that a robot-steered world will have a fixed, predetermined, and mechanical quality to it. In this machine world, it will be harder for specifically human qualities to come forth. That is the fear portrayed in various modern apocalyptic dystopias. A non-flexible, non-heartfelt, non-inspired and un-free machine world cannot begin to appreciate the finer human qualities of being self-directed, having inspired motives, as well as having a compassionate heart. These movies show that we are afraid of becoming the 'slaves' of the machines.

Let's be crystal clear; robots do not have real inner selves. They are executing a dead, mirror-experience of the past, put into action now. Thus, robots have been removed or extracted out from life itself!

When robots are programmed to answer us in a 'compassionate' way, we know that it is fake. A robot world rightfully gives us an eerie feeling exactly because there is no real living heart within a machine that can meet our hearts. Our human life and sense of life, as such, is met with mechanical death when we interact with robots, even if it has a programmed, 'emotionally-toned' way of speech.

Because computer screens can so powerfully steer our attention to where they want to take us, we can thereby become steered from without, not from within. We need to become more aware of the aspect of ourselves that can connect to our own 'flow' from within, not just input from without.

Thus, we need to celebrate our children's own will impulses, both in practical daily living in homes and school as well as when they take power and own their own inner minds and creative responses. If we do not start focusing on developing this aspect of children's education, first in self-created play, later in self-initiated thinking, the self-initiated aspect of being a human may not develop.

Non-fixedness and movement has to do with life. Life has to do with something *new* coming forth. As mentioned, a machine world is an expression of past logical thinking externalized into the gadget in front of us. Creativity and life, itself, would be missing if robots ruled the world, since machines can only reproduce what was programmed already. A machine or computer cannot live, it can only reflect life in its mechanistic way. Since we live in 'fake times', some robots try to *make us believe* that they are basically like humans! Will some folks think it is just fine for kids to have well-programmed robot parents and teachers in the future?

The communal world of the World Wide Web, which combines and externalizes our minds' contents, is dead unless we infuse it with our own lives. The living world around us, in contrast, gives us life. A walk in nature or working in our garden or dealing with our pet will give us health and life. An iPhone won't do that. Playing a piano or doing a knitting project feed us. Not so with the virtual reflected computer world. It takes our life energies to itself and fools us in its lifelikeness. It steals our health away as we sit for hours in front of it.

Living a healthy human life entails exposure to life through our own human senses. Life, health, and sense activities are connected. As educators of our children, we must discover how to give kids life-filled activities. Those life-giving qualities that are missing in our mental-mirrored computer world need to be consciously enhanced, multiplied, and encouraged in our lives today—and especially in children's lives, if we are to remain somewhat healthy humans.

These 'life-enhancing' activities are the new art form. They will balance our lives in these technological times.

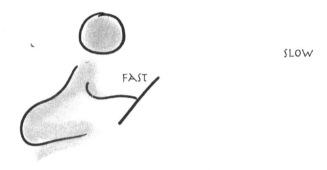

SLOW

FAST

IF THE SCREEN WASN'T FASTER AND MORE ACTION-FILLED
THAN OUR EVERYDAY LIFE, IT WOULD OBVIOUSLY NOT WIN
OUR ATTENTION.

SO, WHICH OF THESE TEMPOS IS CONDUCIVE TO THE WAY WE
WANT TO LIVE?

Summary of Chapter 20

Being an alive human being means to always be evolving and transforming into something we did not know beforehand that we could become!

We are not like a robot, totally pre-programmed, since our invisible self can be 'muse-infused' and creative in the moment with something 'new' and alive.

We have the human-specific ability to overcome ourselves, and rise above our circumstances. Unlike robots, we have an invisible, higher self that we refer to as 'I'. This 'I' is what pulls us up by the bootstraps when we are grown up!

If we are to become fully human, we must have no 'dead' area within us. Our hearts and thoughts must infuse all the deeds we perform. A robot has nothing alive about it. If it appears alive, it is fake.

Robots challenge us to really start to know who and what we are as human beings. It is important to counteract the deadening influences of the electronic world by building life enhancing activities.

21. PRINCIPLES FOR GROWING HUMANS

The essence of being human as we have defined it is developing the capacity for free, balanced, and realistic inner development.

Principles and ways to grow this capacity in children through life enhancing activities are:

- Don't rush around.
- Use art to feed the human heart.
- Allow kids to find themselves through Nature experiences and challenges.
- Grow balanced, inquisitive minds.
- Build capacities for the real world.
- Be in the center of our own lives.
- Build grit.

Rushing Around Inhibits the Human 'Thing'

We must try to counteract the superficiality of modern living. Rushing through a landscape in the car actually teaches us to *not* pay too close attention to what is happening out there! We also learn to *not* care and feel so deeply when we see thousands of movies. Thus sensory overload actually teaches superficiality! This also steals away the caring part of ourselves, because it is impossible to care about everything that is coming towards us. How do we counteract the paralysis of our emotions that necessarily happens with too much information?

We have to allow time and space for our own responses! We have to celebrate our children's 'digestion processes' as they add their own creative juices to the experience they had. We need to look for our children's individualized expression in their reflections on the impression they had. If we rush around never having 'down-time' to digest experiences, the invisible human responses are silenced. Input-time is 'up-time' in our children. Self expression, at a self-chosen speed, is 'down-time'. This may mean 'day dreaming' or just 'poking' at things. Sometimes kids have to get 'sick' in order to slow things down enough for the personal digesting of impressions to happen.

Art Can Grow the Human Heart

When Shakespeare said in the Merchant of Venice that we shouldn't trust a man who doesn't have music in him, he was onto something. The flexibility and depth of heart that can develop when the arts are pursued safeguards a child from becoming hard-hearted and superficial. We have to engage our children in all kinds of artistic expressions so that they can become 'trustworthy' as human beings.

The problem with the 'Hitlers' of the world is that they have no artistic depth and softness, no developed heart-refinement. Mass shooters' hearts are machine-like, like the guns they use. Such hearts are not moved towards compassion because they have lost a certain pulsing life quality. Their heart is 'dead' within them. Artistic expression moves human emotions. For kids, doing artistic things, not just looking at art, practices developing emotional 'muscles' for better movements in the heart. That assures that the heart will stay 'alive'. Art, in its very nature connects us to the invisible and creative aspect of ourselves. Art gives us wings and a sense of freedom within, and can safeguard us from crudeness.

Finding Themselves in Nature

When our children are exposed to Nature and interact with it in ways that include bodily movements, reality checks and balances are developed in them. In addition, as they do this kind of activity kids somehow take part in the full picture of being here on the planet. In fact, for kids to fully take in the reality of this world as a human being, they need to have as many firsthand experiences in Nature as possible. They need to be immersed.

Not only that, concrete, real experiences challenge them and allow them to realize their own real responses as these emerge from themselves. Those responses include developing physical capacities and a range of emotional responses they didn't know that they could have. Virtual existence does not have the same effect.

As kids grasp more and more of their own humanity and get real about his world, they may need to scrape a knee, hike some miles, and help out around the house. Body-exposure 'therapy' is necessary in this century! Being outside teaches them how they can develop skills to survive on earth. This is both useful and very interesting to them. It also builds calluses and thicker skin.

Growing Balanced Minds

If we can infuse wonder and questioning into our teaching, we will help children to develop open minds and we will stimulate individualized activity under each 'thinking cap'. It is a teenager's right to find their own freely discovered thinking, and gradually to come to their own conclusions!

All childhood long, kids need to be stimulated to continually connect and reconnect their thinking, feeling and doing brains. The 'reptile' (doing) brain with the 'mammalian' (feeling) brain with the 'cerebral' (thinking) brain need to be connected in all possible ways through all possible participatory activities as well as reflective activities. Outer activities need to pull and draw inner activities out in us. We cannot be 'inner' the whole day, all childhood long! And we need children to develop capacities in all areas of themselves. If we do not see ourselves acting compassionate, artistic, creative, logical, practically capable, we would not know that we can be those things! We would not know that these personal attributes were in us unless they were allowed some outlet.

Capacity Building

What children, themselves *can do* is what is most interesting to them. This is so, all for a good reason. Kids subconsciously feel responsible for living their own life in the best way possible. Knowing themselves involves finding out what they, individually, are capable of. This is why_capacity building, not knowledge accumulation, is childhood's middle name. And in any case, our internet has already accumulated that body of knowledge for us to click into existence. In contrast, only we, *in our own bodies,* can 'embody' the capacities that are right for executing many specific tasks.

Capacity building is meant here in the broadest sense possible. In the social realm, a bit of every feeling needs to be *lived* into and united with, personally, while growing up. Stories about human suffering and difficulties as well as artistic expressions about human conditions need to be given time. Doing a play, for example, builds social and emotional capacities!

Capacity building also means stimulating curiosity and having kids engage their own problem-solving-abilities in order to awaken their intellectual faculties. Kids need practical tasks in the real world in order to grow their practical capacities for tackling the concrete.

THE STRICT LAWS OF PHYSICS ARE A KIND OF 'BOUND WILL' IN NATURE. IF YOU NEVER ARE IN NATURE, PRACTICING OBEYING THOSE LAWS, HOW CAN YOU KNOW THE RELATIONSHIP OF THE HUMAN TO THE WORLD?

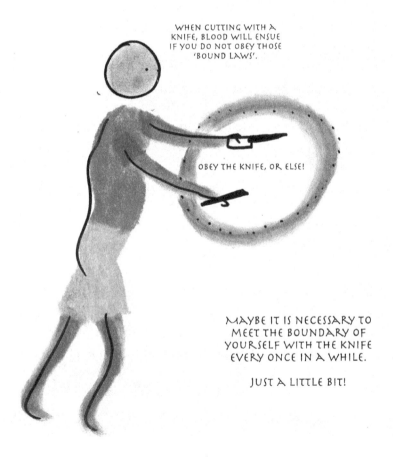

WHEN CUTTING WITH A KNIFE, BLOOD WILL ENSUE IF YOU DO NOT OBEY THOSE 'BOUND LAWS'.

OBEY THE KNIFE, OR ELSE!

MAYBE IT IS NECESSARY TO MEET THE BOUNDARY OF YOURSELF WITH THE KNIFE EVERY ONCE IN A WHILE.

JUST A LITTLE BIT!

These doing, feeling and thinking pursuits enhance the children's sense of being *alive* and *whole* human beings. Because kids are full of growth and life forces already, they experience themselves as living verbs, and connected to this world, when they engage in all the above activities.

Being in the Center of Our Own Lives

Simple but personal and participatory activities of living life on the planet are what is needed to balance our kids' lives among all the fake, pretend-to-be-life experiences that the screens portray. These life-filled activities will put-to-right again our lopsided society's influences.

For example, let's make jam today! Let's pick the berries, rinse them and smash them and can them, and…

When we simply make food, we are giving the most basic human response to things. Food making is culture. And making culture of all kinds is our most human response. When we stop being overloaded, we will gradually start making our own culture, our own play. When we *physically* do things *together* with the people around us, the creative endeavor of social life starts to unfold.

Building Grit

To start being the center of our own lives, we need to realize that we have become creatures of convenience and part of today's convenience culture! And therein lies the danger. We have become dependent on our machines to care for us and have, as a result, become more weak-willed because cars drive us and screens entertain us. But developing grit means overcoming resistance…

So, we have to consciously make life a little harder for ourselves and our children. For a start, we have to stop buying 'convenience foods'. We must start to make our food instead from scratch. Let's put ourselves back into life as action men and women!

And this also means not making life and tasks too easy for our kids. Cutting up vegetables is hard, but it develops 'grit'. We develop the child's emotional depth (feeling) by letting him or her experience both pain and joy. For example, tasting a food that is new can be 'painful', but doing it leads to braver and more nuanced children that have developed emotional grit!

It also means that you do not give everything immediately to a child, but let them 'wait' (have a little pain) before they are rewarded for waiting. We develop the child's own thinking by sometimes presenting them with musings and questions, rather than giving immediate answers. That 'resistance' stimulates their thinking caps to call forth activity from their minds.

The struggle is what matters. These suggestions all allude to giving children opportunities to have *something come forth from themselves*. That something is invisible. It is the will to grasp, to brave and to tackle things.

That will is what we allude to when we sing 'We Shall Overcome'. Overcoming ourselves means raising ourselves above our natural urges, our tiredness, our bored states. It means the coming forth of something 'more' from the inside of ourselves. Overcoming means strengthening our will by exercising it.

For our children, overcoming can be exercised by delaying gratification, by finishing the assignment, when they don't feel like it, etc. To begin with the grownups may need to be right next to the children, steadying them. Children only slowly acquire this specifically human trait of delaying gratification and overcoming their urges with help and consistent steadfastness from grownups.

That is why it is important that children do not have an 'Easy Street' life but are provided with adequate 'substance' or resistance to have to _work through_. This is what is needed for a human to begin to find himself in the human community at large as a member with some personal power.

It is *the struggle* to delay gratification for a kid that builds character. It is *the walking of* the extra mile that builds muscle. It is *figuring out* how to solve a problem by himself that makes a kid learn to trust his own thinking.

This means that *the child is being active*, not the device, not the grownup. Overcoming age-appropriate 'difficulties', in loving environments that support and steady that overcoming-activity, puts the child back in the center of her life as a living verb.

And in that human verb-place a happy and alive kid will be found! That is because a verb is alive and a noun is dead.

Summary of Chapter 21

The primary methods for stimulating the development of the human element in our children call upon growing the individual's own activity, enabling the growth of inner activity, mobility, and strength.

Important means are:
that life is not rushed,
that art is used to nourish emotional life,
that there are plenty of interactions of nature and sensory experiences and challenges,
that learning methods stimulate the human mind's own activity,
that thinking, feeling, and willing activities are intertwined in different combinations,
that children build real capacities,
that they take a hold of their own lives, and
that they build grit.

Though we live in a world of machines, we must take care that we remain the activity-center of our own universe, or our human presence will become obsolete.

THE GENIUS OF THE
SCREEN IS ITS ABILITY TO
RE-RUN HAPPENINGS
FROM ANOTHER TIME
AND SPACE.

WHAT IS ON THE SCREEN COMES FROM
A FAR AWAY PLACE

THAT IS NOT WHAT LIFE ITSELF IS ABOUT. LIFE, AS SUCH,
CANNOT BE TRANSFERRED TO ANOTHER TIME OR ANOTHER
PLACE. LIFE IS HERE AND NOW. LIFE IS NOT A RE-RUN OR
REFLECTION OF ANYTHING, BUT THE REAL THING!

KIDS HAVE JUST ARRIVED HERE. THEY JUST RECEIVED LIFE.
WHY WOULD THEY WANT A REFLECTION OF LIFE AROUND THEM
AND NOT THE REAL THING?

22. INSIGHTS

Being a successful parent or teacher means developing a dynamic insight into who our kids are and how they work. We need to develop appreciation and tolerance for the stages of childhood as our children go through them. We should also constantly reevaluate what things are worth teaching and doing with our kids in the present time.

Here below are a few basic insights into kids and how they learn that can help you appreciate them.

- Kids are not blank slates.
- Kids need your deep respect and reverence.
- Kids can get damaged by us or healed by us.
- The adult they will become is not all up to us.
- Their future is all open and they have an expectant mood.
- They crave a life-filled way of learning that involves the invisible 'grasping' and 'working through' of the material by themselves.
- Everything a kid 'learns' needs to come back out of them with *their own flavor* on it.
- If this 'doing' or 'drawing out' doesn't happen, the teaching we do has no meaning for a kid. The story has to matter to them, personally, if it is going to stick.
- We grownups need to watch and celebrate their emotional involvement, as expressed in their drawings, their essays, and so on.

It's About Transformations

Everything that is going on with a kid is full of life. Life is constantly in a transformation or it wouldn't be alive! The mysterious thing about life is that we experience activities in ourselves dynamically shifting from one paradigm to another! Let me explain what I mean.

We all transform our food into power to work. How did that happen? We transform the experience of goodness from people into trust in life. What we experience in the daytime, for example, is transformed into a nightly 'movie' in pictures as we dream, our heads resting on pillows. Sensory and concrete experiences in our bodies become a 'virtual' dream language which is a totally changed paradigm all together!

We do not understand how all these paradigm shifts happen but they show us that we are not 'input-output' mechanisms as much as we are transformational beings. The more life there is in us, the more transformational possibility there is in us. Kids, being so life-filled, need time to make everything into their 'own' with plenty of down-time. Sufficient down-time makes a kid whole again and it also develops them into an interesting and deep person!

Kids Live Outside Themselves

Living in one's senses means that one lives *into* what the sense organ experiences. You actually live *out there in whatever you experience*!

In previous chapters we described in detail how kids live more in their senses than do heady grownups. Kids have better and newer sense organs than adults. They naturally live more in their sense experiences in a subjective way, unshielded. This is why childhood experiences stick deeper than grownup experiences. We grownups are not so 'fused' to our experiences anymore but have more distance due to our mental life. Our schools propagate that distance by talking *about* the world in order to free us from bondage to it. Children, though, need first to be bonded to and united with their experiences before they will want to distance themselves from them. Kids do not have motivation for hearing about it otherwise. There isn't a reason for them to free themselves from something they were never united with in the first place!

If we fully grasp the intensity of the sense-life of kids, we realize that the outer environment, beautiful or ugly as it may be, matters more to them than to us. It matters more the younger they are. This is because *kids are their experiences*. This must be understood in the sense that they have grown-together with their surroundings. We grownups *have* experiences; kids *are*, in a helpless way, *united* with theirs.

Kids Learn All the Time

Wouldn't it be nice to think that when kids are doing video games or silly stuff on their iPhones, they're not really 'learning '? This is wishful thinking on our part. Children are busy absorbing everything, whether we are instructing them or not. Children have an innate ability to do, feel, and be alive in their learning processes, not some of the time, but *all the time*. Kids' natural state is that they cannot *not* learn, whether they are in school, or playing video games or hopscotch, or watching cartoons, or climbing a tree. Kids learn from everything they interact with.

Kids learn three main things from us grown-ups: (1) who we are, (2) how we conduct ourselves, and (3) how well we understand what *their* needs are in our boundary-settings and rules.

They do not learn that much about the truths and facts we think we learned from life. Kids 'swim' inside their own living development *now*, not in the grownups' reflections and deductions from the *past*. Only as they get older will they want to reflect upon things and hear about other people's reflections with deep interest.

Kids Learn Something When They are Ready for It

The effective absorption of anything for a kid happens best when it is age appropriate; that is, when it meets the timely need for clarification of certain issues in the kid. How does that readiness come about? It comes about partly through bodily developmental changes in the kid, but it also comes about because a kid has had the right sensory life experiences. Kids will need help from adults to reflect on, clarify, and verbalize these experiences.

When we have been fused or enmeshed with some experience for a longer time, we will want to gain perspectives on it. We are, in fact, longing to hear about it from other sources than our own in order to have our own version affirmed and put in perspective. For example: We love it when we as teenagers hear about an angry revolutionary person's biography because we may recognize some of his feelings in ourselves. We also love it when we are in grade school hearing about a greedy-pig that got in trouble, because we know that greedy feeling in ourselves.

Subjective First, Objective Later

Real understanding and true knowledge has two components for children. Subjective learning comes first; then it can grow into objective learning later. Nowadays we aren't giving kids enough subjective learning first to give them reasons for developing objective learning. Objective learning could also be called scientific thinking. Maybe our times would be more science-and-truth-minded had kids been allowed to be more subjective in their experience-field when young?

The learning progression of children described above is *as bound a law* as the laws of physics. How a stone rolls down the hill happens according to the laws of physics; and growing from wanting personal and subjective, to wanting objective distance, also occurs with a strict lawful progression.

Kids need to have a certain amount of real-life sensing and action behind them if traditional school learning is to be meaningful for them. Farm kids of the old had more of that! If kids do not get enough firsthand experiences they find school to be a boring waiting room. Where is the life in school? In the social dynamics with peers in the hallways, of course! (That's where they are *really* learning something, since that is where the action is.)

Nothing Time

If your child is not being entertained, it means that your child is not being steered from the outside in. Their own creative activity is then not being suppressed. We have to remember that this creative activity is tender and requires time to start unfolding. It cannot be rushed!

Children need to be allowed practice-time for steering their own inner activities also in the daytime, not just at night in their own dreams. Kids generally have a dreamier consciousness than adults, and they should be allowed to day-dream for at least part of their day. The playing, doodling, and aimless strolling are all important parts of childhood. These activities let them breathe in amongst goal-oriented pursuits.

This dreaming or playing will not happen unless we stop the barrage of toys that already have agendas, and computer and tablet screens filled with grownup ideas of having fun. We have to stop the rush and slow down their over-scheduled lives. We need to give kids *nothing time* and *nothing space*, so they can unfold their own inner lives with their own 'flavors' and creative processes.

" I AM BORED!"

HOW LONG CAN A KID STAY BORED?
IT ACTUALLY ISN'T THAT LONG BEFORE THE CURIOUS
AND CREATIVE SELF STARTS FIGURING OUT A FEW
THINGS!

MOST PARENTS NOTICE A BIG SHIFT TOWARDS
CREATIVE PLAY AFTER 2-3 DAYS FREE FROM MEDIA.

Kids First, Technology Second

The problems facing our youth now are wake-up messages, telling us that we have put technology and own parental lives first and them second. They are in an existential crisis, sincerely confused about who they are and what they are here for. They have much more anxiety than before. They know themselves less than any other generation ever did.

The iGeneration spends half of their waking life using electronic media and technology. They are an open but insecure and unhappy generation. They were guinea pigs for the iPhone life, and something went wrong. Living through an iPhone isn't a better life, after all.

We need to understand what comes first for humans. As kids grow into this world, they need to have experiences that prove to them that they are connected to this place and that they fill a purpose here. Distancing them from the world is not what is appropriate in this phase of life! Childhood, simply, is the wrong time to go into a far-away and reflected world!

We adults have been mesmerized with our own technological advances. *This* is now possible and *that*, too! But technology distracts children from what's really important, namely their *own* relationships to actual things!

Development From the Ground Up

Bosses are better bosses when they know how to do all the jobs they are going to boss other people to do. A boss should have submitted previously to the bound and practical rules of those jobs and should thereby totally understand them.

Childhood is about getting inside all jobs possible, both through play and work. This makes children deeply and truly understand the world and how it works, from the ground up. Children need to try out many types of jobs and challenges—knitting a sock, whittling a spoon, taking care of another life, running a mile or two, and serving a meal that they cooked. Those concrete activities are interesting and meaningful to children, much more meaningful than we grownups seem to think!

Rules and Structure

Kids are most harmonious when there are rhythms in their days and weeks. When the day has rhythms, then little kids, through habits, 'know' what to expect, and they feel safe. When kids never know what's going to happen, they will be clingy! If every bedtime routine is the same, it calms the nerves of a kid. If every mealtime has the same rules for sitting together saying a grace, for example, it soothes and makes life easier for kids. And kids love to be warned about what's coming: "In five minutes we'll need to leave the playground." "Tomorrow mommy will be home with you."

Grade school kids respond to unbendable rules in the context of social settings. "This we do here, and other things we do there." They totally accept structure once there is a rule about it. It makes things fair, too—a super-important ingredient for grade-schoolers.

Kids are newcomers to this world and they need an ordered world so they can feel secure as they begin to tackle things. This gradually changes as kids become teenagers that require more excitement. When a kid has had a safe childhood, they *should* want something new when they are teenagers.

If, in contrast, childhood has been unpredictable and unstable, with no consistent rules and consequences for how to behave, kids become nervous. If your parents were bendable, and you were allowed to be a brat when you were a kid, you will be anxious about having kids of your own.

Children actually get freed from their bad behavior when they learn to be good and helpful humans. If we do nothing about their obstinacy and instead leave them to their yucky moods, we are telling them that one cannot do anything about a yucky mood. But on a subconscious level they learn how to turn a bad attitude into a positive one when we show them how to do that when they are young! That is done by *having kids do something that is better.* This can happen because we have the power over what kind of activities they do. This is parenting in a nutshell.

If you utilize the parental authority that is given to you, naturally, you can help turn a yucky mood into a sweet one. This can help your kid to budge and do something positive. Your child will now like themselves much more and have a good self image as a result. They also learned how they, themselves, can turn bad into good later in life. This was a tough-love lesson in optimism for life, actually.

Enforce the Rules

We grownups now should be able to tell ourselves to control our lusts and desires and to rise above our laziness. A kid secretly hopes that we have a few tricks up our sleeves to help them learn self-control and appropriate behavior. Rules and consistent consequences are part of learning to behave!

Writing your house rules down and 'externalizing' them by hanging them on a wall or fridge depersonalizes them. It gives them a fairer, more objective feeling because they are extruded from the subjective parent figure!

Summary of Chapter 22

Children are not little adults but function according to their own laws. Here are some insights into how kids work and learn:

Initially, children need to live in subjective, real experiences before they can develop objective capabilities. Hence many educational efforts are misplaced and result in school time not being in sync with the learning needs of children.

Rushed life, school, and media life can hinder children from having the primal, real experiences they need to obtain to be healthy, and also can hinder the digestion of real experiences. Enabling children to have enough 'nothing time' helps them to develop their individuality.

Wise use of structure and rules can help provide children with stability, protect them from too much of the outer world, enable a balanced emotional life, and develop their life of beneficial habits.

23. GROUNDING KIDS

Coming Into This World

When a kid is not grounded, he is not well. Parents have to be on guard if a kid is in an 'out-of-themselves' or 'ex-carnated' state.

In general, when groups of kids arrive on the farm, pouring out of their cars, I would have to characterize them as being ungrounded. I am often worried that we might have an accident on the farm. But then we get to work, digging, fixing and responding to the farm's work-demands. When they leave, these same kids are grounded. By the time they leave, I am no longer so worried about accidents! What happened?

It is simple. Doing stuff with the ground grounds us all! The secret is the ground itself and our limbs acting towards it in a purpose-filled way. If we got grounded, the job is well done. If the kid did a bad job, we grownups would have them do it over again to do it 'right'. The grounded-ness of a kid is, literally, to be seen in the pudding they made, the sock they knitted, or the deep hole they had to dig for a tree to be planted. The 'proof' of *a kid being on the planet* is in the 'pudding' or thing they accomplished.

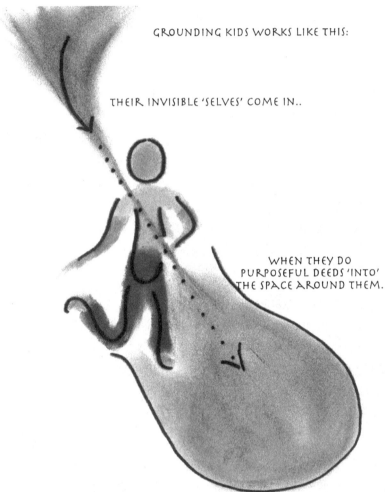

GROUNDING KIDS WORKS LIKE THIS:

THEIR INVISIBLE 'SELVES' COME IN..

WHEN THEY DO
PURPOSEFUL DEEDS 'INTO'
THE SPACE AROUND THEM.

WHEN KIDS ARE 'OUT OF THEMSELVES', LET THEM SWEEP
THE FLOOR OR ORDER THE BOOTS IN THE HALLWAY.
WHEN YOU HAVE APPROVED KIDS' CHORES AND TOLD
THEM "WELL DONE!", YOU WILL NOTICE THAT THEY ARE
MORE WELL 'IN' THEMSELVES.

IF WE SIT STILL OUR WHOLE CHILDHOOD, WE CANNOT
GET 'GROUNDED'. WE NEED THE GROUND FOR THAT!

In times past, grounding a kid meant being punished because the kids had broken the rules set by the parents. The kids were pinned to one piece of ground, their rooms or houses. Prison, likewise, is meant to be a "go to your room and think about it" place for grown-ups who don't understand how their actions affect others. Strong and firm boundaries calm and ground them, supposedly.

For a kid, 'going to your room' was seen to be a place where one could come to oneself after being lost to oneself. A little quiet time made 'alignment with the world' good again. But going to your room is one thing. Actually doing a good and needed deed can set the wrong, right again. A kid needs us to help their deeds turn good again.

The mystery of how our invisible selves come down to the planet has to do with outer physical circumstances demanding something from us. We have to be careful and awake. We help kids to come 'in' when he or she has to learn to coordinate his or her own actions according to physical as well as social laws. Each time there is a bruised knee, he or she gets reminded of those laws. Each time someone gets angry at a child or glad because that child did something nice, the child learns social laws.

All this bumping up against physical and social concrete realities makes kids wake up, gradually. Waking up entails that the attention moves from a dreamy/blurry sense of self to the 'crisp' outer world. The kid's attention is on something outside their body, awake to the realities and needs of something in their environment.

This is how the incarnation process works: becoming aware and developing the personal skills to respond appropriately to the physical and social environment around us. We incarnate when we are drawn out of ourselves to do something *for* someone. In this way, our needy surroundings work as the big *Educator* by drawing us out in an appropriate way. We call this '*Needucation*'.

It can be said that when we 'incarnate', we go *out through ourselves* into this will-activity, responding to practical or social needs. We are then living through ourselves, outside ourselves physically. We are living outside our bodies in space, filling it with our invisible will! When the ancients said that we have to lose and forget ourselves to find ourselves, they are pointing to this process. We 'un-self' to tackle the world, and as a byproduct we get to know and 'find' our self.

In today's world we sit in cars and rush all over the earth at tremendous speeds. We are not present in looking and sensing what is around us. Instead, we are in our own world, our own car-bubble, likely with the radio on. We are all rushing around like nervous mice in our own bubbles. We are, literally, un-grounding ourselves many hours a day on top of our fast-moving tires. Truth be told, we do not have that much choice either!

So, because our culture cuts us off from the Earth, we *need* practical tasks. Simple, practical jobs heal us and bring us back to the present.

A kid that is 'out-of-himself', is helped if a teacher touches his shoulder when talking to him. The kid usually listens a little better with that little bodily touch. A kid that is 'out-of-himself' comes into himself when he draws pictures, hops on the line without mistakes, or cuts up vegetables with a sharp knife. The deed he is doing wakes him up to earthly reality. We all come *into* ourselves when we scrape our knee or have pain. We went over 'the line' and the pain woke us up. When no pain is ever experienced, kids are not sure that they exist!

As humans, we loosen ourselves in laughter and descend deeper into ourselves when we cry. Therefore when a kid cries due to exhaustion before bedtime, it is actually a good preparation for going to sleep! A kid cannot go to sleep if they are too excited, 'out there' and 'wired'. Doing computer work before bedtime doesn't help any of us to go to sleep. Going for an evening walk, however, settles us all down. Walking is an activity that grounds us in the most primal way!

When kids have too much free time for 'hanging out', we need to have them do some purpose-filled work that connects them to the community around them. That grounds the kids and makes them happy. Conversely, when kids have too much work we need to give them a breather, some unscheduled time. That bit of nothing-time can be all that is needed for the kid to not get sick.

All life long, we breathe in and out of ourselves by oscillating between sleep and awake states. We concentrate but then need a break. We sleep in bed but then can work well in the day. The better we sleep, the more awake and effective we tend to be during the day. As good educators, we will notice when the children's state of effective attention-giving is used up and they need recess.

Because our high-tech homes and schools do not offer enough grounding activities for kids, we need to reinstate some. After all, an ungrounded kid doesn't learn much! He may be waiting for that accident to happen that finally will ground him.

Grounding kids into physical space on this planet depends on there being a meaningful reason or purpose for the action. Sports are good, but not enough. When there is a *necessity* at the other end of the deed performed, it grounds us more than if the deed is play! This is why kids usually need to do their chores first, and then afterwards they can play more productively.

Kids need to do the heavy first and then the light thing. Besides teaching 'work-ethic', it also evaporates away their ungrounded state. As we have said, an accident will not happened as easily after a job is well done.

It is up to us to notice when it was enough grounding activity or 'work'. You adjust the bar to where you see it produces a balanced kid. Remember, the task done to your satisfaction proves the kid's well-grounded state.

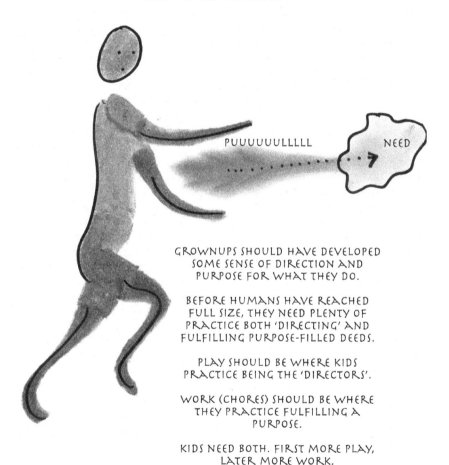

A PERSON NEEDS SOMETHING BEYOND THEMSELVES TO LIVE FOR.

WE ALL NEED PURPOSE. PURPOSE HAS TO DO WITH A NEED THAT MUST BE 'FILLED' OR 'MET' IN THE WORLD AND A PERSON THEREFORE RESPONDING TO IT.

PUUUUUULLLLL   NEED

GROWNUPS SHOULD HAVE DEVELOPED SOME SENSE OF DIRECTION AND PURPOSE FOR WHAT THEY DO.

BEFORE HUMANS HAVE REACHED FULL SIZE, THEY NEED PLENTY OF PRACTICE BOTH 'DIRECTING' AND FULFILLING PURPOSE-FILLED DEEDS.

PLAY SHOULD BE WHERE KIDS PRACTICE BEING THE 'DIRECTORS'.

WORK (CHORES) SHOULD BE WHERE THEY PRACTICE FULFILLING A PURPOSE.

KIDS NEED BOTH. FIRST MORE PLAY, LATER MORE WORK.

'Out to Lunch'

Being 'out to lunch' is the opposite of being helpful for others. We have to be *in ourselves* in the first place in order to *go out* through ourselves to do a chore or help another person. That is exactly the therapeutic effect.

A chore, like sweeping the floor, is on the outside of a kid. I reiterate: a chore done well shows us kids who are well in themselves. A chore done poorly shows us kids who were not all the way into the job, kids who were 'out there' somewhere else with their attention or lack of it. The chore is what helps kids to gradually arrive *here*.

The message in doing a chore is, "Wake up to the here and now." Tending to our physical environment is healing to all kids. It is especially helpful for kids who are 'out there'.

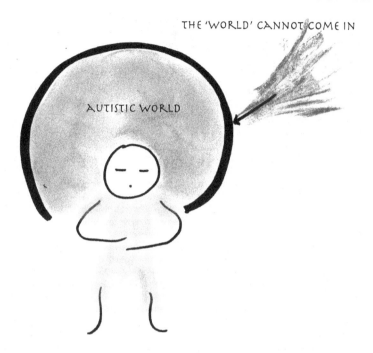

THE 'WORLD' CANNOT COME IN

AUTISTIC WORLD

WHAT IS GOING ON WITH ALL OUR AUTISTIC
KIDS?

ISN'T IT THAT THE OUTER WORLD'S REALITY
DOESN'T PENETRATE INTO THEIR INNER WORLD?

THESE KIDS HAVE SHUT THEIR SENSORY WORLD
OFF TO VARIOUS DEGREES. THEY SAY 'NO THANKS.
MY INNER WORLD WILL DO.'

DID WE MAKE A WORLD THAT WAS TOO MUCH
FOR THEM TO HANDLE?

Grounding an out-to-lunch kid is simple: make him do something purposeful on the ground and let him finish the task, if possible. By finishing the task, namely, you give him the pleasure of also letting him *know that he was here*. Since the job was completed, it is now visible to everyone how competent he was. Sweeping the floor, arranging shoes in the hallway, or setting the table can be easy tasks to begin with. You must make sure there is a mastery feeling for the kid at the end, not necessarily perfection for you. Check if Johnny isn't less 'out to lunch' after the job was well done. Again, we get grounded by being pinned to a task here on the actual ground.

'Difficult' Kids

Sometimes we have a battle of wills with a child. That is a difficult thing for ourselves and we like to say the kid is 'difficult'. This could have many reasons. But comfort yourself with the fact that having a 'spineless' kid is actually worse!

When a kid is difficult, it could plainly be that his temperament is very stubborn. That simply means that you, too, need to be strong and not give in. You have to match that will! If you do not, this child will get the eerie feeling of being in charge. That is deep down very scary for them to be dominant in a world that they just arrived in. The grownups have been here longer than they have and should know how it works here! A willful child getting their way all the time will result in their will growing weaker for life, not stronger. When their strong will meets the right resistance, consequences, and form, they become more self-confident and sure of themselves as a result. Steiner said that the will gets stronger by getting resistance, just like any muscle will.

Irrespective of what the kids say, they will become happier and feel more secure when the universe/parent is obeyed. Your job is to make consequences heavy enough so the child ends up choosing to do the right deeds. This is not exactly fun for you, but you are in charge of teaching the truth of how the world works. The world has harsh rules. Being a namby-pamby parent, will teach the lie that the world is namby-pamby. You are then setting your kid up for a harder life than necessary.

Summary of Chapter 23

Many kids are not grounded but they become grounded when they do constructive acts with their environments.

We incarnate into ourselves when we are drawn out of ourselves, through ourselves, to do something for someone or something.

Simple, practical tasks heal us and bring us to the present. Giving kids a 'Needucation' means drawing kids into themselves by serving the needs of the world outside themselves.

'Out-to-lunch' kids can be helped by pinning them to tasks and making sure they complete them well.

'Difficult', willful kids must be brought into line with the world using firm but fair consequences. Their will is actually strengthened that way.

24. GROWING SANE CITIZENS FOR A SANE FUTURE SOCIETY

The truth is that if kids are not grounded in the physical and social reality, they will live in an untruthful world that fits their personal will instead. We humans must *not* be free to make the world obey us. We *cannot* tell the world that there is no gravity or that the other person's feelings don't matter. During childhood, we should learn to know *our own personal place* in the bigger world that is outside our bodies.

Raising kids means arranging the circumstances surrounding them to give them true experiences of their place and their power in the universe. With a willful child this need is out in the open, but with a seemingly undemanding child it also needs to happen. Sneaky and hidden weaknesses in kids need to be brought to light, and dealt with too, and that can be harder!

Becoming Aware of Others

In previous chapters we described that the healthy maturation process is the *moving of your inner focus* from self-absorbed self-experience in childhood to realizing that the needs of others are also out there. I call this process developing 'other-centeredness'.

We all needed a lot of push and pull to learn to take other people seriously. In the old days kids lived in cramped quarters and they were taught to have manners. Manners are 'other-centered' ways to behave that make social life more pleasant for everyone. The sooner we learn to be 'other-centered' the happier a society is.

A democracy is built upon the 'other-centered' idea that all opinions and all people, as such, should be seen and be respected. That is a great and valuable ideal that we also try to adhere to inside our family structures. Everyone should be validated, including our children who are going through their various stages. In our culture, if things aren't happy, we go to therapists. That is an attempt for an individual who hasn't felt heard to be seen all the way. Even though you are the 'umbrella' under which your child lives, they still need to be seen and heard and understood by you.

The World Wide Web was supposed to give us a world-wide consciousness. It has had the unintended consequence of making us sometimes less awake to the here and now with each other. It has also, in this unintended way, made us be able to cocoon each into our own mental worlds.

We can have the world all *on our own terms* more than ever when we are on the net. We only want to hear the kind of news *we* want to hear, see the films *we* feel good about watching. We want to have the thrills and unreal fantasies that give us pleasure. We don't need to adjust for the 'other'. We get less practice to adjust to anything but our own likes and dislikes. As a consequence, children, especially, can avoid waking up to the 'other'. This problem has been enlarged by the internet.

In addition, with Facebook our kids see new on-the-screen versions of themselves showing what they *want* to be, not necessarily who they really are! We don't see others for the nuanced and complex people that they actually are, but more who they 'dream' of being on their selfies. Fake reality has become more real than reality itself, at times, because more of our time is spent with it.

Our world is not as simple as before because the boundaries of self and others have been blurred. Nevertheless, we all feel better when we are respected and seen for *who we really are*. In our present society how do we get to know and learn to respect *the other* in a real way?

Practical social awareness of everyone else is something we never feel that we have totally down. We can always get better at it. Technology has taken away the learning about 'the other' as a *complete entity*. This is because only a part of a person gets 'through' the devices, not the whole and real person. Often it is a projection of the acceptable parts of a wannabe person that has been 'cropped'. None of us can mature as a human being without actual reality. And the truth is that none of us will want to live unseen, as a fake, for the rest of our lives.

Building Sanity

One part of being sane is knowing that the world of one's mind is in sync with the reality we live in together. Little children used to grow out of their fantasy worlds by having strong experiences through their truth-telling senses and hands. This physical *reality check* is available now in much small portions. The distinction between physical reality and fantasy versions of the utopian possibilities is blurred for an insane or unreal person. The danger with too much fantasy time and screen time is we can literally get 'out of touch' with reality.

If sane people did not take care of insane people, the latter would perish quickly. Children need guardians for this very same reason. They are on their way towards getting real about things as they become experienced being here. Kids learn about sanity, or the truth of how things work here, experience by experience. Learning to distinguish between fantasy and truth needs to be given room and time, and it needs to be taught to our children, especially during the grade school years. It doesn't happen on its own.

Summary of Chapter 24

Growing sanity in our children and future society means instilling practical social awareness, other-centered habits, and a healthy sense of reality in kids.

Gaining these habits goes beyond instructions from parents or teachers. Concrete experiences with reality have to teach them, too.

25. REAL EDUCATION

Developing The Brains Of Children

With our educational methods and tricks, teachers try to give kids activities that will influence their brains to become better instruments for their mental lives. Let's be clear, the *purpose* of the brain is not for to be a great brain per se; it is, instead, to provide the possibility for better human *life performance*. A smart brain will be able to respond to the outside world intelligently. That is what matters.

The growing and developing brain gets formed as a response to a back-and-forth interaction of brain and environment. That brain was given to us via heredity. The brain becomes a "report card" for how outer circumstances and stimuli met the nerves given to us by genetics. The actual indentations and forms in the gray matter are 'grades' of how well school and home drew, pulled, and pushed at the child and made the internal nerves work in response. We, literally, have 'marks' from all that activity!

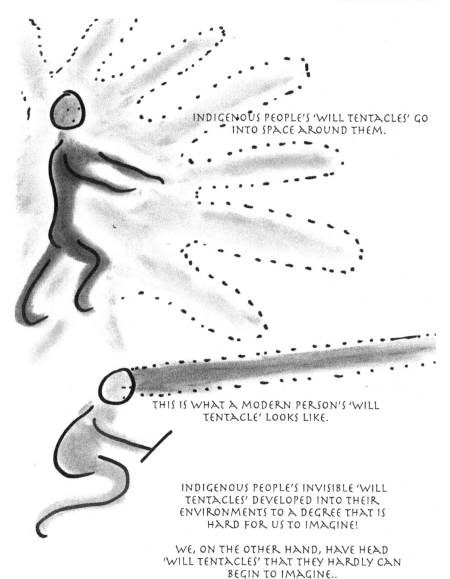

INDIGENOUS PEOPLE'S 'WILL TENTACLES' GO INTO SPACE AROUND THEM.

THIS IS WHAT A MODERN PERSON'S 'WILL TENTACLE' LOOKS LIKE.

INDIGENOUS PEOPLE'S INVISIBLE 'WILL TENTACLES' DEVELOPED INTO THEIR ENVIRONMENTS TO A DEGREE THAT IS HARD FOR US TO IMAGINE!

WE, ON THE OTHER HAND, HAVE HEAD 'WILL TENTACLES' THAT THEY HARDLY CAN BEGIN TO IMAGINE..

Let's be clear once again: The self of the child isn't the brain. Though the brain is a material portal for the self to enter through, the actual self is invisible. Through the times prior to ours, we have called this invisible self the Spirit.

We experience the invisible self *through* deeds done, feelings had, and thoughts entertained. The more we do, the stronger we feel and the clearer we think, the more we experience ourselves as an alive, invisible entity manifesting into the material world. The well-developed brain assists us in having this fulfilling life-experience since we can enter so well into the world through the grey matter in our brains.

But here's the thing—the brain isn't the only 'portal' through which the invisible self enters. The senses of our bodies, have plenty of nerves too, and are also channels through which the self can have 'experiences'. Though the sense organs are physical organs, they give us non-physical experiences that we call heavenly, beautiful, ecstatic, yucky, and the like. And, we know that people who sensed something directly through their own personal sense organs will have 'learned something', reaching a deeper layer of themselves than someone who experiences it only secondhand.

Deep Learning

Our learning institutions do not presently value this 'learning by doing' or 'deep learning'. If they did, kids would be taking field trips all the time! If 'deep learning' could be easily tested, maybe we would value it more. Because it has to do with the subjective effects of learning, it is hard to measure objectively.

We have created schools that are suited for reflecting upon life. But the kind of information-transfer that goes on there will not reach the deeper layers of our brains unless we already had a number of personal experiences. The knowledge acquired there will not push and pull much on each child, as each one of the kids does not matter that much in such a school setting!

Having a kid experience milking a real cow, like we do in our farm program, is a hassle. How much easier, cheaper, and efficient to show the kids a sanitized film-version of where milk comes from to a big group of kids. In our farm programs, we sometimes meet parents who have a hard time understanding why we bother. ***We believe in 'deep-learning'!***

We really believe that children have that right to, at least once, experience a bunch of things first hand. We believe that the bodily nervous system needs to convey experiences to the brain in order for the brain to be fully indented and formed the way it was meant to be! We believe that the children's brains will not be formed as they should be without also that actual real-life experience through the senses.

We believe that children, more than adults, need to have time and places where they can develop a rich sensory life and not only a barren 'screened-in' life.

Slow Down And Smell The Roses

We all know the "use it or lose it" rule. If we do not use some talent we have, we may lose it more or less. This is the case with our senses, too. They will atrophy and not grow into their full potential if we do not use them intensely.

Childhood is especially equipped to develop the senses by drawing their interests into sights, sounds and smells. Those sense organ nerves are as important as the brain nerves for experiencing the full intelligence of our world! Our senses were made to match and meet this planet. 'This sensory education' happens best in calm environments where there is no rush, no urgency or 'fight or flight' mood.

The sensory 'will tentacles', as described earlier, have an anemone-type of slow pace for developing that needs to be considered. We do not participate here on the earth with an open nervous system that is 'learning' unless we feel somewhat safe.

When we are in a safe situation we slowly connect the dots and the intelligence of our two 'brains', the introverted one as well as the extroverted one. The introverted one is inside our skulls and the extroverted one is dispersed in our entire body as 'sensors' for the external world and for our world of digestion.

We need both sets of brains to get an education that will make us healthy and adjusted. This duality within us performs polar opposite functions: actual sensory experiences and then the virtual, mirror-experiences in our minds. Isn't it obvious that we need both to be a complete human being?

Summary of Chapter 25

The brain, as we think of it, is an instrument for the Spirit of a child. It is formed by the environment and heredity.

However, there are other brain-like functions associated with the senses distributed around or body and in our digestive system.

The invisible Spirit enters more deeply into the body of a child when there are 'deep learning' and 'doing' experiences on Earth associated with a rich sensorial life.

Modern schools are mostly concerned with reflections of life. This does not affect the child so deeply as do such experiences in which the child fully participated.

If the senses are not used they will atrophy.

Real education should address both subjective and objective ways of learning.

We need to assure that children first obtain personally sifted-through experiences. This will build the motivation and inner need for reflection as the child matures.

26. EDUCATIONAL OBJECTIVES AND BUILDING CAPACITIES

The Path Toward Gaining Mastery

There can be no shortcut to gaining mastery of things. Extensive work or practice must be done before a person can build a house from scratch, cook a meal well, or do a math problem.

The need for hard practice before gaining mastery puts the student in a humble place within the bound laws of mastered deeds. We will never learn to be realistic and good at something unless we have plenty of personal, concrete experiences with the subject. The more we have mastered, the more it took from us to get us there.

Work that produces results affirms what we can do. We deduce who we are from that. Practical wherewithal is mastery of our physical surroundings. It grounds our invisible self to the earth, as we have mentioned.

ACQUIRING MASTERY OF SOMETHING EQUALS FINDING
ONESELF IN THE WORLD

MY ENERGIES
COMES OUT HERE

THE 'WORLD'
MEETS MY
ENERGIES

WHEN I INTERACT WITH THE CONCRETE WORLD, MY INVISIBLE
'WILL TENTACLES' GET CORRECTED BY THE WORLD OUTSIDE MY
BODY. WHEN I LEARN TO COMPLY WITH THE STRICT RULES OF
THAT WORLD, I EXPERIENCE MASTERY.

In the grade school years the activities that *build a capacity in the child* are what is ultimately meaningful to a child. Any capacity acquired means the child's own will has been refined, strengthened, and 'pruned' effectively for a certain task. The child itself is made useful for one specific area of life, whether it is chopping wood, running, sewing, or something else. A capacity means the large and fine motor skills have been acutely developed. The bodily nerves became well connected within the body to tackle the world without.

Unlike building up a body of knowledge, building capacities has something to do with the child himself, the child's own motor skills. The latter connects the individual child correctly and intelligently to the world that he or she landed in, one set of nerves at a time. Thus capacity-building also builds kids' inward sense of purpose and a sense of self.

Building capacities and acquiring mastery takes lots of repetitions to become anything, so we must not be afraid of repetitions and more repetitions with kids!

Real Social Skills

This repetition goes for social skills as well. Think about it: Good social habits are formed from the outside in, by the surrounding culture. Early cultures understood how important it was for kids to learn to respect things. We, in our hectic world, have often forgotten that. Respect not only ensures social harmony, it also is very good for the kids themselves. Why? Because building respect actually teaches them the true picture of their places in the social universe. The truth is that the kids aren't running the show. Should we pretend that they are?

Today we must *consciously* build places and situations that will allow respectful and meaningful social capacities and attitudes to solidify into habits for life. We need to be the form-givers for social behavior. For example, "This is how we behave when we visit someone's house." In today's world, we are asked to be the consistent habit builders for 'other-centeredness', which is manners. 'Good manners' is the same as social mastery.

By providing enough time in physical space and time with your kids, you help them dip into 'un-cropped' physical reality as well as non-altered social reality. When kids dip into the real thing, their capacities form as a natural response. We cannot be so sure of that when our kids are only in virtual 'reality'.

Engender Interest and Critical Thinking

Interest and curiosity are expressions of intelligence. If our kids aren't interested, something isn't being received. To be interested is the natural state of a kid! That is the state where invisible-interest tentacles naturally 'grow' out of the child. But the sensory overload kids are living in puts

179

brakes on the development of kids' own interest-tentacles. Everything comes towards a kid, but very little is asked *from* him.

Our educational challenge is to help kids get many personal experiences that mature them while stimulating them to be inwardly interested in the world. Unless a kid is interested, school learning, or any learning, cannot be effective.

When kids go to school, many of them waste their time there, since they aren't motivated. They have different questions than those the school addresses. Actually, it can be even worse for these kids being in school than just that they *waste time*. These uninterested kids are day by day building *negative* habits of fooling around and doing purposeless things. If we take their lives seriously, we have to admit that they are, literally, *practicing* being without a purpose!

Observation skills and critical thinking are in embryonic stages as the child pokes around as a two year old. Kids have curious and questioning interest-tentacles coming out of them in their openness, all the time. At this stage they are working on developing the prerequisite to critical thinking which is expressing open curiosity through their senses. However difficult these guys are to watch, we must not extinguish this state! How do we grow this open and interested inner state? It is certainly not by putting a sensory-poor screen barrier between them and the world.

Little kids live in a magic place, a wonder-place. This changes as the children get into the grade school years and learn to 'think' a bit about the world. But we can continue to grow capacities for intelligent wonder and openness by not letting the curriculum be always a 'finished product'. In the younger years, developing the capacity for critical thinking is stimulated more by open-ended descriptions of things from an adult.

Our tests for kids in science should be about making accurate observations and deriving the most pertinent questions, not about who can best remember and regurgitate other people's findings. Questioning things, in general, opens the mind up. Having a ready-made answer tells us that the thinking process is over! We want to develop a lively inner life, right?

We have to remember that tests are mostly for grownups to find out how effective *we* were with our content-transfer methods. They mostly do not indicate the deeper thinking-capacities kids will walk away with into their own lives. Testing kids in high school can give kids some comparative self knowledge that is useful for them, but before puberty, testing as such is grownup centered and not at all what kids need! Grade school kids should be 'tested' on all kinds of capacities built, not for knowledge.

Crystal clear observation skills and critical thinking are capacities that can be gradually developed through junior high school. At that age we should have the kids describe things accurately and ask them questions. As one enters puberty, this activity is 'healing' for them exactly because their bodies are changing so rapidly. Thinking accurately helps them find something to hold onto!

Making good and accurate observations and developing probing questions takes more inner activity by the student than spitting out factoids. It can be excruciatingly difficult for kids to observe accurately! Good teachers of this age group are often very good at 'putting the mirror' up so the kids can see the truth for themselves! The kids walk away from such classes with new faculties they grew within themselves.

As kids enter puberty, they are able to take more initiative in their thinking life. As they question things, their mental capacities 'grow'. This critical thinking lay dormant through all of childhood.

Grade school years are the time where relationships develop. Kids are naturally not so critical. Criticalness in puberty is an expression of having some newly found distance to things. A grade school kid doesn't need this 'distance' because they need to find themselves *amongst* things.

Indeed, it is so: A younger child is still in need of being part of the tapestry-of-life. Therefore the desire to 'feel distance' *should* lay dormant and not be woken up in a child during its early years. That feeling of separation is painful and not productive when we are still 'fastening' ourselves to the planet.

You do not want to force a plant to produce a fruit earlier than it should! It is the same for children in regard to becoming autonomous from the fabric of life. Little kids still need the fabric to build themselves up. However, as puberty arrives, producing the 'fruits' of thinking and questioning *should* become a habit. This is, after all, the only way a young person can 'free' themselves from everything too familiar!

Balance Truth and Imagination

Some things in our minds are non negotiable—logic and mathematics, for example—but focusing only on these aspects of life can make life very sterile. Sometimes 'engineering minds' can be perceived as boring! There is a place in life for imagination. We want ourselves and our children to have imagination, too. Fantasy or dreaming toward something that is beyond what is already here is what makes us interesting and alive in our minds.

Little children have endless imagination, naturally, because they are full of life! As we mentioned before, a kid before 6 or 7 will not fully know a lie from a truth! We mustn't blame a small child for lying. We simply reiterate what is the truth, but do not blame them for their imaginative version of how it happened.

This changes as the grade school years arrive and they must learn to speak the truth, to not steal, etc. But a small child feels totally misunderstood if he is blamed for being untruthful. The 'reality of the truth' arrives slowly as the outer circumstances wake the child up bit by bit and the first phase of childhood is complete. The first phase lasts until the change of teeth at around six or seven years old, as mentioned.

Kid-play benefits the child *more* when it is self invented, not planned out by grownups through suggestive messages in toys and on computer screens. The self-directed imaginative process develops creative minds in our kids. We sorely need that developed imagination in our humans to find new ways of tackling problems in the future. If we cannot even make visions of what and how things may be better, we will surely not be able to make those things better!

It is freeing to be creative in our activities, but it is also freeing to be truthful in our thinking. Kids must gradually learn when to be accurate and when to be imaginative and inventive. When you sit in court being questioned, it is not the time to be inventive; when you are 'think-tank-ing' with other people, it is.

Our times have turned many grownups into gamers, not scientific and truth seeking thinkers. We can wonder if these folks had enough imaginative play when they were kids, since they still have this need for play to such a degree as grownups. Or was it that they never got the opportunity to learn to enjoy the freedom-feeling that self-initiated thinking can give?

Give Purpose To Everything

The hungry baby at its mother's breast is bonded to its mother by the necessity of survival. The father/son bond came naturally when they had to tame horses to plow the fields together. Nowadays, families living in homeless situations may have stronger bonds than the rich who do not need each other to survive. If you want to develop psychological and social bonds together, then *do things together*, purpose-filled things.

If you want to get a closer relationship with someone, find things to do where the ingredient of *depending on each other* for accomplishing something is present. Situations where we all have to *pull together* to accomplish something have bonding effects between us. Our personal wills have to align together for something that is bigger than ourselves to happen.

An 'Outward Bound' experience, where you may die if you don't collaborate with the group, may be necessary for an individual in extreme cases when all meaningful human connection is missing. Life itself used to be outwardly bound—outer boundaries with physical consequences—all the time. Now we have to consciously put boundaries of various sorts back into childhood in smaller installments so kids can wake up, bit by bit, to their purpose of being on this planet together with others.

That sense of purpose for kids has to do with learning to give the appropriate responses to everything within the contexts they are in. Give kids opportunities to *practice those responses* to a variety of things. Someone must run to Grandma, who is sick in bed, with a warm drink—an obvious need that draws the kid to help. The animals got out of the fence, and someone must figure how to get them back in. We will not have clean clothing tomorrow, unless someone will do the laundry.

As was mentioned in previous chapters, kids need to see themselves as having power to solve many problems. Something is awoken in kids when the real need is actually there! An invisible will-impulse (that we never knew about prior to this incident) is 'drawn out' by a real need.

Having a too-perfect childhood, a too-perfect school experience may actually atrophy the kids' abilities to become problem-solvers and initiative-takers. It is important that kids have experiences in after-school situations where *they* can improve this world. Having small degrees of difficulties, can in this way draw out their inner resources. When kids see themselves filling a gap, they feel purposeful. They find themselves as they 'take on' a necessary place. It feels good to be needed! It ultimately means that they are important. Time must be allotted for kids to have such experiences.

In the future, more of our jobs will be replaced by machines. The whole world, theoretically, could run on its own. It becomes a social problem when people lack purpose. If a person's childhood has been virtual, the need for achieving personal purpose may seem huge and unsolvable. But if children are constantly learning to meet needs and also exercising their creative sides while growing up, they have a much better chance as adults at re-making their lives when difficulties or catastrophes hit. That is simply because they have practiced being active and it is now a habit to be active.

All these life experiences will make them trust that the right actions will emerge from themselves when needs arise. They simply will know that they can do whatever it takes.

Con fidare means 'with fidelity' in Latin. To have self-confidence, lit-erally means that one knows that one can trust oneself to do many things. It points to being able to be loyal to oneself and one's ideals of how to be a human. It points to having a *strong will* and tenacity to endure because one knows one can do what is right, whatever may happen. We want kids to have self-confidence, not just a *feeling* of self-esteem that may be fake and not based on reality.

Build Positive Relationships

We are what we are due to the *position* we have been given by our circumstances. We become who we are as a result of our relationships to humans, place and work. Each one of us is in the center of our own circle, and we have to learn to relate in all directions, physically as well as socially.

A person has social capital when they have developed positive relation-ships with family and friends that are supportive. We need to consciously help our children to build their social capital. Kids need other kids, but even more, they need stable relationships with grownups who see them for who they are. Grownups need to look for those relationship-possibilities that can enrich our kids' social capital. It is our duty for the future generations.

Each kid is different. We need to help each one to find the human connections that will help him or her to live their life in a realistic way, not in a too wishful way. Honest relationships, where people learn to depend on each other, help children to build their sense of self. Learning to show respect towards peers and grownups provides kids the social habits that will be useful now but even more so for their lives ahead.

Summary Chapter 26

As kids learn to respond to needs in their environments, they are finding a place for themselves on this planet. They thereby develop wherewithal which is the capacity for gaining mastery over their physical and social surroundings.

Building capacities starts in grade-school. It has to do with building motor and social skills and interest in the world and, later on, critical thinking.

Education should strive for a balance between truth and imagination. Childhood, especially in the grade school years, is the time to learn to distinguish between the two.

After-school educational experiences should encompass purposeful social and practical deeds that build real self-confidence in kids. This means that time must be allotted for in-the-world activities!

Gaining feedback from adults outside the home makes kids become authentic and it rescues them from an unsure state of mind.

Initiatives from the kids themselves make them resourceful. Consequences of their decisions teaches them about who they, themselves, are in a way that gives true self confidence that can never be taken from them.

27. HOW TO DO IT, IN A NUTSHELL

Set Boundaries Around Device Use

Watching movies in small amounts is not what is so terrible. The problem has to do with the quantities of movie watching or video games we indulge in. If there is no downtime to digest this content, it could just be one sensory overload experience after another for your kids.

We need to allow ourselves to transition back to the pace of real life. We need to let ourselves come off the caffeinated, action-life of screen media. If we don't, this screen-experience will induce 'more-more' feelings, the not-being-satisfied feelings. That sensation is the addictive tendency developing in us. Kids aren't awake to this addiction-making tendency, and neither are many grownups. This, of course, is why kids need to have parents that are aware and set boundaries so that the children do not develop addicted personalities.

Like adults, some kids have more addictive tendencies than others. If your kid is one of these types, he or she may tolerate little screen time before becoming difficult to bring back into the here and now. You will know.

This entails that when a kid is doing video games, or social media, or watching YouTube, you are observing how it is affecting them, i.e., whether your kid gets more or less active by watching. Let's say he is learning a dance move from the screen. This obviously will make him better at dancing if he practices it. But if he just watches for hours, and he is passive and dull on the inside, you must put boundaries on this activity for him.

Your simple guideline is: _which_ is being more active here, *the kid* or *the device*?

If the answer is the device, you must rescue your kid! You are in charge of your kid becoming a verb so they can live *their own life* again! That rescue obviously involves setting boundaries around this titillating influence! If the answer to the above question is that the kid is becoming more active by learning a song or dance-move or he is acquiring some piece of information that helps a project he is doing, then everything is in order. In either case, modern parents have to take on this new boundary-setting job, and it demands their wakeful vigilance.

This new parenting paradigm makes your job as a parent hard because these influences are affecting your children in your very own home. On the other hand, your home should be where you are able to exercise control over all influences! This is not meant to be theoretical, take this power concretely! At least *here*, in your home, you can determine and be responsible for which world your kid will live in—the physical, tactile one or the virtual one.

In addition to educating the grandparents to stop giving an overload of candy to your kids, you also have to forbid their providing hours of screen time for them. That is not together-time with grandparents! Convince them about the culture you want your kids to receive and make them aware of the active one or the passive one, the real one or the virtual one.

All that said, remember that being a fanatic about no movies isn't teaching your children what you want either! After a good movie, just make sure you all talk about it and share feelings about it all. There is no purpose to guilt when your kid has overdosed on media. It is our role simply to do it better next time.

YOU MUST SET BOUNDARIES AROUND
MEDIA USE FOR YOUR KIDS OR:

IT WILL TEACH THEM THAT LIFE IS FASTER
AND MORE THRILLING THAN IT ACTUALLY IS.

IT WILL TEACH THEM THAT THEY DO NOT
MATTER, MOSTLY.

IT WILL TAKE AWAY TIME TO BE TOGETHER
FOR REAL.

IT WILL TEACH THEM ABOUT A FAKE,
WANNA-BE SELF, NOT THE REAL ONE.

IT WILL MAKE THEM MORE THIN-SKINNED IN
TACKLING THE CONCRETE WORLD.

Give Nature-Experiences And Nothing-Time

Since so much can happen on the *looks-like-life* computer screen, you must become a warrior for the real and sacred life of your kids. You have to be the conscious provider of the planetary-experiences for your kids—even if it makes you feel like you are "shoveling shit against the tide," as my father-in-law so observantly put it.

Teach the kids to sew, whittle, cook, fish, do carpentry, garden, tend animals, jump rope, and to go for long walks in nature with you or someone else.

Not only can kids feel scared of the physical world if they never have interacted with nature, but they also do not have a clue about the rich life they are missing. This ignorance, as we have mentioned, is a new type of sensory poverty.

Every minute of every activity that our kids are doing, something develops for what they will become in their lives. Every activity executed by children makes them find themselves, either in a virtual or physical or social context. Where they find themselves is where they make their homes. We make their home turf by choosing for them their verb playing field. This goes for allowing boredom too. Please remember that boredom is the beginning of finding the creative fount within!

BEING BORED AND BEING IN NATURE WILL
DO THIS TO YOUR KID:

IT SLOWS ALL INTERNAL RHYTHMS DOWN
TO A NATURAL PACE.

IT OPENS UP THEIR MANY SENSES.

IT DEVELOPS THEIR NATURAL CURIOSITY.

IT MAKES THEM GET CREATIVE.

IT IS REAL LIVING, NOT FAKE.

Have Kids Do Chores <u>With</u> You

Aside from allowing children to have original experiences and time to play, parents and teachers have the responsibility to help them practice *being* participants and contributors. This may not be easy. Our desk-centered, adult work-lives hardly offer opportunities for our children to practice being helpers. We also think that helpers should be paid, and that child labor is bad. This book, I hope, shows you new perspectives on that!

Have you seen how happy kids are to be helpers? I have. Manual, simple, and life-preserving old-fashioned work activities such as cooking from scratch, harvesting garden produce, and tending to animals incorporate kids into life. If you have done these activities with kids, you know that they *love* to do these things *together* with you, especially those activities that end with something good to eat for everyone.

This aspect of kids' education is what has been called here 'Needucation.' We are 'drawing out' the children's responses to real needs. Satisfying the need should 'explain' to kids that they actually matter here on earth! This activity produces an active human being who can fill a hole, a gap, a need. The person who is responding becomes a verb; not a passive onlooker, but an active and alive human being. They connect to their surroundings and build invisible 'roots' into it.

Naturally, for 'Needucation' to happen for kids, we must have an environment that has a few actual needs present. A sterile apartment with only a microwave will not do. It is necessary to have needs that a kid can be successful at meeting.

The demands of homesteading are perfect for meeting a grade school kid's level of accomplishment possibilities. Kids can learn perfectly well to milk the cow, weed the garden, handle the chickens, and even a two year-old can gather eggs. They experience that *they* affect the world, that they have purpose as a member amongst all the creatures on the planet.

For this reason the old-fashioned farm setting was a perfect 'Needucation' setting, teaching a kid that life is not all about them. Everybody was empowered as capable doers, as participants and contributors, in the agrarian society.

It can be like pulling teeth to get a kid away from the mesmerizing video game to fold laundry. This resistance makes it necessary for you to know why you still need to teach your kids to help out.

Whatever you make your kid do (or not do) is a gift (or lack of) to your kids' future spouses and bosses and everyone with whom they will have a relationship. You may seem mean, and you certainly don't like yourself in the role of teeth-puller, but you have to do it for your kid. You have to pull these teeth! This is about your kids' future. It is about *them* becoming capable and likable.

Many people say that it takes about three days of kids being away from media for them to be easier to be around, which means they notice you and other things more. They have slipped back into living in a more sensory-aware place and aren't so intensely in their fast-running minds all the time. It is easier to ask them to do things in the here and now. This three-day rule is the good news!

Since making kids responsible for things around them is often harder now than in earlier times without gadgets, we need to develop this new awareness of why it is so important to teach kids to help out. *The awareness of their surroundings has to be consciously taught* to kids today. As they are put into roles of service for both people and place, it helps for you to know how valuable this 'place-based' education is.

The ramped-up stimulation of electronic media is truly like caffeine for us all. Folding laundry and sweeping floors takes the time it takes. It seems like slow motion when we come off of video games! Waking up to the physical reality of earthly needs, like chores that are necessary to do in the home, draws your kids' attention back to the earth-pace which is our actual and meant-to-be home-cosy pace. It is not the consumer culture's frenzy of 'more for less' but instead the mindful and aware place revealing to us all that, really, 'less *is* more'.

You will find that doing house chores together is great binding glue for a family. The community feeling that develops when we pull towards a common goal together arrives amongst family members. The chores need doing anyway, and now we did them, and we can 'feel' the lovely clean abode we have created. We could call cleaning our house *together* work therapy or family therapy. The inner aspects of the 'house' get cleaned in the same go.

Don't expect little kids to do chores alone until they are much older. This is the point—it brings us together. It is the together-part that is missing in this world for kids. This was so natural in earlier times, and no consciousness needed to be shed on these daily tasks. But nowadays, since the convenience culture dominates our culture, we need to consciously know how community and family bonds are made if we want to have them. If we want a together-feeling, we must 'together-do'!

DO CHORES WITH YOUR KIDS BECAUSE:

IT TEACHES 'UNALTERED' REALITY.

IT TEACHES OTHER-CENTEREDNESS.

IT GIVES FORM TO THEIR ENERGIES.

IT GIVES PURPOSE.

IT GIVES A FEELING OF BEING TOGETHER.

IT GIVES A CHANCE TO DEVELOP CAPACITIES.

IT GROUNDS KIDS.

IT DEVELOPS STAMINA WHEN REPEATED.

IT DEVELOPS A SENSE OF RESPONSIBILITY.

IT GIVES TRUE SELF-CONFIDENCE.

Summary of Chapter 27

Utilize 'Needucation' opportunities.

For deciding on how much electronic media watching should occur, use the guideline:

who is more active, the kid or the machine?

The new parenting paradigm requires that you:

1. Limit gadget-activity.
2. Go outside and risk being bored.
3. Do purpose-filled tasks, together with your kids.

28. MAKING NEW CULTURE

These three guiding principles, turn gadgets off, go outside and do jobs together outside and in the house, will already have bonded you to each other in a new way. When the work is done, or the walk is finished, you will not end up sitting and staring at the wall. You will have already become enlivened by the useful and practical things you did. This new life style will leave you time and space to do and create culture together as a result. You will start talking to each other, interacting and playing, making and creating. There are actually many creative things inside grownups that want to see the light of day!

Restructure Celebrations

What is a birthday party for kids these days? Taking them to a movie or other grown-up-made event with a grown-up-made cake? Kids are recipients of birthday products made by adults in birthday businesses. Kids are practicing being a consumer and a recipient.

What if, instead, children helped grown-ups make their own cakes, and the kids that came to the party made their own pizzas to eat? That would be celebrating the verb-children, the doers that the children are, rather than our capitalist businesses. That would be a child-centered party, not a grown-up, show-off party. Yes, I know, it is more work for you. But, really, it doesn't have to be so complicated or too elaborate.

There is nothing more significant for your children than that you create culture *together* with them. Let's again clarify what happens in a child when we tell or read a story to them in comparison to a screen experience:

1. For the story to become a rich experience for the child, they must become creatively active. They must make mind-pictures from the word symbols they are hearing from you. In short, your reading engenders more inner activity in the kid than a movie can.

2. When you read the story, a living and interesting person (you) and your child both make imaginations, but the two sets of imaginations are somewhat different and thus individually, by necessity, filled with each of your life histories. In short, there's a more personalized version of the story within the child and yourself than a movie could ever be. Your two inner lives are interacting and influencing each other!

3. It is a *together-for-real* experience with the grown-ups, not a *together-alone* experience of having to pretend that you are together with someone, since the truth of a digital-media experience is that it is just you and your dead device that are together. If that is not how you think about it, that is due to your own imagination! There is more of an actual integrated, life-connecting, life-sharing experience when you and a kid are being *together-for-real*.

Putting it plainly, a sensory together-for-real experience has to do with being alive now. Who, actually, really wants to miss 'the now'?

Sharing inner cultural musings and experiences of multiple kinds is the ultimate quality-time we can have together. We are connecting with the 'muses' that come through each of us.

Real life *with you* is better for your kids than any reflected, secondhand version of it. Never doubt that. Seeing you be creative with their toys, or drawing pictures for them, or reciting kids' poetry makes the kids feel understood and also teaches them to love the very best things that life has to offer. This heightens the quality of life for both you and your kids.

Summary of Chapter 28

The main thing about making family culture is that no manual should tell you what to do. You need to be free to see what comes out of yourself and your children as you interact, without anything between you.

Nothing should direct or block or screen the direct 'flow' of your creativities. Culture is what humans naturally do as a response to everything they experience on earth.

It has to do with sharing life together and it doesn't have to be very advanced.

Go for it!

AFTERWORD

Chris, a student I taught for six years in the Waldorf school, met me again now as a grown man. I was curious: "What did he remember from his school days?" I thought for sure he was going to tell me about some of the plays we did or class trips or something else wonderful I had helped him experience. Instead he didn't hesitate: "I repaired the vacuum cleaner that one time." For Chris it wasn't about what I had given him, but what instead *he* had given the school!

If we take Chris's message and the message of this book seriously, we will want our children to arrive here on the planet in the way Chris tried to tell me—in his case, the vacuum cleaner way. He found himself in this world *more* through repairing a broken vacuum cleaner than through Mrs. Goldstein's wonderful teaching. Lesson learned: Do not give the children a too perfect world!

If it meant more to a student what *he* could give the school than how wonderful the school was, maybe it is time to put that meaning back into children's childhoods. We grownups are in charge of creating opportunities where the kids experience themselves as if they matter. But let us not do it in a fake way. Let's not do with a virtual pet or an expensive play-dough kitchen set!

Let's do it where the kids make the *actual* food that *actually* feeds our *actual* bodies, giving us *actual* strength. We have to look around us and let the children try out at least what they *can* take on. Pet care, house cleaning, card-to-grandma writing, lawn mowing, etc. This is not child labor. It is, instead, opportunities for stepping into this world!

We will in the future look back at our times and wonder why we put kids in buildings without windows and in front of screens with reflected pieces of the past flickering in front of the their eyes. Asphalt school yards will then be replaced with some nature where 'free-range' children can be climbing a few trees in small and safe community settings. We will then have understood that *learning* for children has to do with finding out about themselves *just as much* as finding out about the 'world'. How can they find out about themselves by being in storage chambers under constant exposure to other folks' findings?

We will then have understood the *interactive part* that children are dying to live! We will have understood that children are, literally, *dying* to be alive! That means being a Verb. That means not being just a figment of an imagination in the Virtual. For Chris, this meant **HE** came in, and that broken vacuum cleaner was the means by which it happened. Amen!

ABOUT THE AUTHOR

Bente Goldstein, born and raised in Norway, is a Waldorf teacher. She has run immersion programs for kids on her organic farm in Elkhorn, Wisconsin, for decades.